Profit from the Positive is a phenomenal book because it suggests small changes that make a huge difference. You'll learn to ask yourself—What is the smallest action you could take? What if you preview performance? What could you do in five minutes?—and the results are extraordinary. It makes the difference between you at work and the best version of you at work. And it's contagious—as my colleagues see me implement what I've learned from the book, they are putting the ideas to work for themselves.

—Debbie Newhouse, learning and development manager at Google and author of *The Magic Seed*

I have two pieces of advice for any startup founder—be prepared for very little sleep and read *Profit from the Positive* from cover to cover.

—Thomas M. Davidson, cofounder and CEO of EverFi, Inc.

In their book, *Profit from the Positive*, Greenberg and Maymin offer innovative ways for transforming a team, a department, even a company, to be more productive and profitable. They have turned some traditionally held notions on their heads, replacing them with ideas that turn stumbling blocks into stepping stones. Better yet, as a business leader, you won't need any capital outlay or long-range planning to implement these tools—today.

—Greg Tranter, EVP, CIO, and COO of The Hanover Insurance Group

Don't go to work without this book! *Profit from the Positive* is a revolutionary, science-based road map to business success. If you want to amp up your success, follow Greenberg and Maymin's unique prescription for driving phenomenal business results through the development of extraordinary employees. Get this book for yourself and every member of your team!

—David J. Pollay, author of *The Law of the Garbage Truck*

There are so many good and useful business and leadership books available. But this book is different! The authors cut to the heart of leadership mindsets that can drive results and create a positive and energized workplace. If you are a leader or aspire to be one, *Profit from the Positive* is indispensable reading.

—KEVIN MCCARTHY, president and CEO of Unum US
and EVP and COO of Unum Group

Profit from the Positive is full of realistic, creative, practical, and effective strategies for leadership in the post command-and-control business world. It is a transformational handbook for leaders, teams, and organizations.

—JOHN P. TARPEY, COO of Balfour Beatty Construction, US

Greenberg and Maymin have written a must-read on how to power yourself, your team, and your organization with easy to read and easy to implement strategies. As Aetna's chief culture officer, I am applying many of the concepts, best practices, and action steps within our culture transformation efforts.

—LAURIE BRUBAKER, CCO of Aetna

A great read! The research on how our moods and emotions as leaders influence our team's productivity struck home for me. Being aware of this is more important than most of us realize. I found the techniques to neutralize a negative mood enormously helpful.

—LESLIE ASHFORD, AVP of executive development
at MassMutual Financial Group

Rarely do you find a book that tackles today's most pressing business challenges with such sound research and practical advice. Maymin and Greenberg have done it. They present more than thirty deceptively simple strategies that should be required reading for every leader, manager, and HR professional. *Profit from the Positive* delivers an amazing gift—a mindset and toolkit that will revolutionize the way you work and lead.

—JESSICA AMORTEGUI, director of global
talent development at VMware

This book is engaging, enjoyable, and practical. Especially intriguing is the notion of turning performance reviews into positive events, borrowing from sports psychology by positively visualizing the year ahead and setting up the conditions for success!

—DEBRA PALERMINO, EVP of human resources
at MassMutual Financial Group

At a time when we are all trying to find ways to do more with less, *Profit from the Positive* comes to the rescue with practical advice and tools that are easy to implement and immediately impact the engagement and productivity of your workforce.

—HEATHER THOMAS, senior director of global
human resources at SNL Financial LC

Profit from the Positive is a must-read for managers at all levels. Using case studies from their coaching experience, Greenberg and Maymin demonstrate how to avoid costly hiring mistakes and create an engaged workforce—and they have the data to prove it. *Profit from the Positive* is written with the needs of today's world in mind. The practical and proven tools contained in this book, combined with its timeless wisdom, will inspire you for years to come.

—LAURA A. BELSTEN, president and CEO
of the Institute for Social + Emotional Intelligence

profit
from the
positive

PROVEN
LEADERSHIP STRATEGIES
TO BOOST PRODUCTIVITY
AND TRANSFORM YOUR BUSINESS

profit *from the* positive

MARGARET H. GREENBERG
SENIA MAYMIN, PhD

NEW YORK   CHICAGO   SAN FRANCISCO
ATHENS   LONDON   MADRID
MEXICO CITY   MILAN   NEW DELHI
SINGAPORE   SYDNEY   TORONTO

1 2 3 4 5 6 7 8 9 0 DOC/DOC 1 9 8 7 6 5 4 3

ISBN 978-0-07-181743-1
MHID   0-07-181743-3

e-ISBN 978-0-07-181744-8
e-MHID   0-07-181744-1

Design by Lee Fukui and Mauna Eichner

Library of Congress Cataloging-in-Publication Data

Greenberg, Margaret H.
  Profit from the positive : proven leadership strategies to boost productivity and transform your business / by Margaret Greenberg and Senia Maymin.
      pages cm
  Includes bibliographical references.
  ISBN 978-0-07-181743-1 (alk. paper) — ISBN 0-07-181743-3 (alk. paper) 1. Leadership. 2. Organizational effectiveness. 3. Performance. I. Maymin, Senia. II. Title.
  HD57.7.G7435 2013
  658.4'092—dc23

                                                                        2013009859

Requests for permission to make copies of any part of this work should be emailed to book@ProfitFromThePositive.com.

Parts of this book appeared originally on PositivePsychologyNews.com as excerpts and can be found at www.tinyurl.com/profitposts.

Illustrations by Jaime Raijman
Jacket photograph of Senia Maymin by AJ LeVan

McGraw-Hill Education books are available at special quantity discounts to use as premiums and sales promotions or for use in corporate training programs. To contact a representative, please visit the Contact Us pages at www.mhprofessional.com.

To Marty Seligman and Chris Peterson, for awakening our passion for positive psychology

—Margaret and Senia

To my husband and best friend, Neal, for his unwavering love, support, and encouragement

—Margaret

To my mom and dad, Zina and Zak Maymin

—Senia

CONTENTS

PART III

Putting It All Together

Foreword

Profit from the Positive is one of the most practical and accessible business books I have read in years. It is rare that a business book compels you to action right away. Once you finish reading *Profit from the Positive*, it will influence your behaviors that very same day.

When I speak with managers and leaders, they share a few common challenges, but what really keeps them up at night is the constant challenge of growing their businesses. One way they grow their businesses is through engaging employees and customers. While most of these leaders know they have a lot to learn about the best ways to engage people, they lack the time it takes to keep up with relevant discoveries.

In the fields of leadership and positive psychology, a remarkable amount of research has emerged over the past decade. There are countless new findings that will help you continue to improve your ability to lead. *Profit from the Positive* translates all of this research more clearly than most of the business books on the market. While the body of research from the new field of positive psychology has been growing, figuring out how to apply these findings in business has been a challenge. This challenge led Margaret and Senia to put the best ideas to the test in their coaching work with executives, managers, and entrepreneurs. In *Profit from the Positive*, they share proven tools and techniques you can apply to your business—large or small.

What differentiates this work from other business and leadership books is its practicality. *Profit from the Positive* has been written and structured with a busy leader in mind. Margaret and Senia distill the essential findings from all of this research in a clear and crisp way accompanied by memorable stories and interviews.

Profit from the Positive is a rare business book that is deeply credible *and* compels you to act right away. If you put its tools and techniques into practice, you will become a more effective leader.

Tom Rath

Introduction:
You've Tried Everything. Now Try Something That Works

You've streamlined processes. You've restructured. You've sought customer and employee feedback. You've done team building. You've even paid out bonuses, thinking that a little more in your employees' paychecks will make them work harder and longer. But it's still not enough. You're constantly challenged to grow your business, increase productivity, and improve quality—all while reducing or keeping budgets flat. What's a manager to do? Hire an A team? Rarely do you have the luxury of picking your own team, and even if you do, you still don't know how well the team members will work together. You've tried everything. Now try something that works.

POSITIVE PSYCHOLOGY WORKS

Profit from the Positive: Proven Leadership Strategies to Boost Productivity and Transform Your Business is a practical guide for business leaders and those who aspire to positions of leadership, executive coaches, and human resource professionals. We translate findings from the new science of positive psychology into succinct, actionable tools that can be applied immediately without spending a dime or hiring an expensive consulting company.

Positive psychology is the study of what constitutes excellence in individuals, communities, and workplaces. It incorporates the study of productivity, resilience, motivation, emotions, strengths, team dynamics, and more.

Despite its long evolution, people usually date the Internet back to 1995. Similarly, even though its roots go at least as far back as Aristotle's writings about the good life, positive psychology was officially launched in 1998 when Martin Seligman took the helm of the American Psychological Association (APA). Yes, this field is younger than the Internet.

Since Seligman and his colleagues launched the field, over 10,000 research papers have been written. In academia, that's an astounding amount of research in a short period. The media took notice of this research explosion and started running stories that sometimes included inaccurate sound bites. This is important: *positive psychology is not positive thinking*. It is not about saying a gratitude mantra while turning lemons into lemonade. Positive psychology researchers seek answers to questions every business leader wrestles with:

- How do I increase productivity without adding to staff?

- How do I get my team to collaborate or step up its game?

- How do I motivate people to perform at their very best?

Many of the findings from positive psychology are not yet readily available to the public. Research is published mostly in academic journals, and the practical applications have not been fully tested. Additionally, MBA programs are just beginning to integrate positive psychology into their curricula. Consequently, few business leaders have been exposed to the new science and fewer still are able to extrapolate the appropriate applications.

That's where we come in. Before starting our own consulting businesses, we both began our careers by working for several large corporations: Margaret in human resources and Senia in finance. In addition, Senia founded three technology start-ups.

Our paths first crossed at the inaugural class of the University of Pennsylvania's Master of Applied Positive Psychology (MAPP), program, which was created by and cotaught by Martin Seligman. Since graduating from this program, we have been translating the relevant research into practical applications for the executives, business owners, and teams we coach. We have helped implement the tools and techniques in *Profit from the Positive* at Aetna, Hanover, MassMutual, SNL Financial, Unum, VMware, and dozens of other companies and technology start-ups. With our clients who were willing to experiment in order to grow, we found more than 30 ways to boost performance and transform their businesses. This book is a result of that work.

Many successful business leaders are already using positive psychology tools whether they know it or not, and you may be too. Each time Cindi Bigelow, president of Bigelow Tea, reminds her managers that they can't afford the luxury of a bad day, she is emphasizing the effect emotions have on a team's productivity (Chapter 3). He may not realize it, but each time Zappos.com's CEO and author of *Delivering Happiness* Tony Hsieh congratulates an employee for satisfying a customer, he is using the FRE (Frequent Recognition and Encouragement) method to improve productivity (Chapter 6).

HOW THIS BOOK IS ORGANIZED

We polled dozens of clients, corporate leaders, and entrepreneurs to discover their most burning questions about running their businesses. Those questions form the basis of the book.

Profit from the Positive is divided into three parts. Part I (Chapters 1 through 4) focuses on you, the leader, and the four mindsets you must cultivate to be successful: *productive, resilient, contagious, and strengths-based*. Part II (Chapters 5 through 8) centers on applying positive psychology research to team and common business practices such as hiring and engaging employees, conducting performance reviews, and running meetings. In Part III (Chapter 9), we show you how to begin implementing these tools today.

Each chapter begins with what's not working. We realize that this doesn't sound very positive, but we're sticking to what we said before: positive psychology is not about positive thinking. What's not working is the business case for why a new approach is needed.

Next, we translate the most relevant positive psychology research that can affect either productivity or profits. After each piece of evidence, we offer specific tools—all research-based, practical pieces of advice—that you can apply to yourself, your team, and your business. We bring our tools to life through case studies from our own business and coaching experience as well as narratives by successful business leaders.

Our hope is that you will recognize a bit of yourself in many of our stories because you have encountered similar situations in your professional life. Please keep in mind that we have changed the names of the protagonists in our stories to protect our clients' privacy.

We end each chapter with a summary of the Key Takeaways and a handful of Reflection Questions. A summary of all 31 tools in *Profit from the Positive* can be found in Appendix A. In addition, a summary of each chapter, followed by group discussion questions, appears in the Reading and Discussion Guide at the back of the book. We'd be delighted if you used *Profit from the Positive* for your next workshop, course, conference, or book club. Additional questionnaires and other resources are in Appendixes B through F and are also available on our website ProfitFromThePositive.com.

Whether you lead 3 employees or 3,000, *Profit from the Positive* is for business leaders who are looking for tested methods to grow, improve, and transform their companies. Even if you don't manage or lead others but are instead an individual contributor or coach who must rely on influence, you will find the advice in *Profit from the Positive* highly relevant and easy to implement.

We hope you enjoy our book from cover to cover, but we understand that you're busy, and so we've made it easy for you to start wherever your interests or burning questions lie. Open the book anywhere and begin the journey. We purposely made the research and practical applications bite-sized so that you can dig into any section, perhaps during your morning commute, and implement those tips after lunch. We're confident that you will find something you can use today to profit from the positive. Enjoy the ride!

Margaret and Senia

PART I

It's About the Leader

n this section, we focus on you, the leader. We begin here because we believe you cannot effectively lead others until you can lead yourself. Leadership, however, is a broad topic with countless opinion-based models, competencies, and qualities that can make your head spin. In these four chapters, we've distilled what you must first be able to do yourself before you can even think of getting others to follow you. Of course, what we recommend is backed up by science.

After reading this section, you will be able to do the following:

- **Get more work done without working more hours** (Chapter 1). For example, did you know that you cannot break a bad habit, but can replace it with a new positive habit?

- **Bounce back more quickly when things go wrong** (Chapter 2). For example, did you know that in tough times being a learner is more effective than being an expert?

- **Exert more influence** (Chapter 3). For example, did you know that the higher up the ladder you are, the more your moods can affect the productivity of the people who report to you?

- **Do more than solve problems** (Chapter 4). For example, did you know that one way to improve your team's productivity by nearly 40 percent is to adjust the way you react to bad news?

In each chapter, we share with you practical tools you can implement today, all of which have been tested and are backed up by the latest research. Go ahead; turn the page and get started.

THE PRODUCTIVE LEADER:
It's More Than
Time Management

Seventy percent of Americans report that work is a significant source of stress, according to the American Psychological Association. Additionally, Americans on average work eight hours more per week than their German counterparts, yet they are no more productive. For the last 50-plus years, sociologists have been asking people to keep time diaries of their activities. Surprisingly, people report only one more hour of free time today compared with 1965. We're busier than ever, yet we seem to be accomplishing less and less.

We already know about setting priorities, making to-do lists, and accomplishing big goals by breaking them into smaller chunks. However, many of us undervalue setting aside time to plan our work. We know what we should be doing, but sometimes we can't seem to get out of our own way. In coaching hundreds of business owners and executives, we've found three common drains on our productivity: we're overworked, we multitask, and we procrastinate.

We're overworked. One of our clients, Paul, heads a data services department that provides support for offices around the world. He's not only overworked, he's exhausted. "We have seventeen offices located on three continents and operating in eight time zones, which makes it really hard to unplug," he laments. Paul is not alone.

Nine to five has been replaced by 24/7. In an informal survey of a dozen Millennials, Margaret asked, "What does nine to five mean to you?" The most common answer? The score of the previous night's ball game.

For most of us, 40-hour workweeks are a thing of the past because of two colliding forces: a global economy and access to technologies that allow us to be available around the clock. We used to think that having operations on both coasts was a challenge. For businesses that operate globally, even scheduling a conference call can be a challenge. No matter how you juggle calendars, someone has to get up in the middle of the night to participate.

Paul describes a typical day: "I try to force myself to leave the office by 7 p.m. at the latest and limit the amount of work I do from home. This is a big shift from my prior roles, where I would work from 7 a.m. until 8 or 9 p.m., go back to work at midnight, and stay until 5 a.m. That said, I think I fail on a pretty grand scale in terms of maintaining a balance between work and the rest of my life."

Even if your business operates domestically, chances are that you're still overworked because of constant access to technology. Our clients often complain about the time it takes to keep up with the barrage of emails that assault their in-boxes. An 11-hour workday is the norm for our client Ellie, who leads an integration team for a newly acquired financial services company, and those 11 hours are merely the time she spends in the office: "I typically leave work around 6 p.m. so I can be home in time to have dinner with my husband and kids. Then, once the dinner dishes are cleaned up, the homework finished, and the kids are tucked in, I log back onto email for a few hours before going to bed. The next day, it starts all over again."

Yahoo! CEO Marissa Mayer stated previously, "I do marathon email catch-up sessions, sometimes on a Saturday or Sunday. I'll just sit down and do email for 10 to 14 hours straight." Mayer describes regularly working 90-hour weeks and taking a one-week vacation about every six months.

We multitask. While our client Eddie waits in line to pay for his turkey sandwich, he scrolls through his in-box on his phone and listens to a voice mail. "You forgot your change," the cashier yells as Eddie makes a mad dash for his office, arriving barely in time to log on to a 12:30 conference call with his boss and the rest of the team. After announcing himself, he hits the mute button and replies to a couple of the emails. In the middle of the third email his cell phone beeps, announcing that he has a text message from his golf buddy. As he's typing his reply, he hears his boss: "Eddie, are you there? Eddie?" He unmutes himself. "Ah, yes, I'm here." "What ideas do you have to solve this problem?" his boss asks. Ideas? Eddie has no idea what the team has been discussing.

Many clients tell us they are so busy that multitasking is the only way they can accomplish everything. They participate in conference calls while driving, do Internet searches during meetings, and respond to emails while talking on the phone. Multitasking has become associated with being more productive, but this couldn't be further from the truth. The biggest hit to your productivity from multitasking is what we call *flip-flop costs*. It takes effort to flip-flop or switch from one focus to another. In fact, we lose up to 40 percent of our productivity from flip-flopping between tasks. In a typical eight-hour day, which we know is no longer typical, that translates into three lost hours.

JUST LIKE AT THE MOVIE THEATER

Martin Seligman, one of the founders of positive psychology, has a phrase he sometimes uses about 15 minutes into a keynote speech: "As a psychologist, I can tell that about half of you are listening to me and half of you are having sexual fantasies." Part of the audience usually erupts in laughter, while the others look around bewildered, wondering what they missed.

Margaret uses a similar technique to kick off her workshops. "For the next two hours, let's imagine we're at the movie theater." Margaret smiles. "Please turn off all electronic devices." Then Margaret goes on to inquire whether attendees are familiar with the term *absent-presence*. A few heads nod. "It's when we are physically present but mentally absent, like when you call into your weekly results meeting, then put your phone on mute while you check your in-box." Knowingly, guilty smiles appear on almost all the faces in the room.

A study conducted in 2007 calculated the loss of productivity and innovation resulting from social media interruptions at $650 billion annually. Answering emails as they come in has been estimated to cost U.S. businesses $70 billion a year.

Imagine that an email pops up while you're drafting a presentation. You answer it and then go back to the presentation. Next, a text comes in, and you reply. When you return to your presentation, research shows that it will take you longer to regain your focus and finish your work than it would have had you stayed with that one task. That's a flip-flop cost.

When we don't flip-flop between tasks, we often get our best ideas. For example, Jeff Taylor, founder and formerly Chief Monster of Monster.com, got the idea for his online job board company while he was sleeping. In fact, he claims that he's had some of his best strategic ideas when doing nothing at all, not while multitasking. Executives we coach often tell us that they found the solution to a particularly nagging problem after a jog or a swim.

Flip-flopping can also have a hidden cost: damage to your reputation. Remember Eddie? He later told us how embarrassed he was at not being able to contribute to the conversation: "I looked like a jerk to my boss and the rest of the team, and lost some of their trust and respect, which will take time to earn back."

We procrastinate. Being productive is more than simply practicing good time management techniques. Sometimes we procrastinate the way Tracey does. Tracey is a busy director for a financial services company. She travels the country helping satellite offices implement a new product portfolio. At the start of the new year, Tracey's boss gives her a special project: develop a phase II rollout strategy with estimated resources. It is now almost the end of the first quarter, and still nothing. Tracey knows that her boss is waiting to see her plan, but she wants to use what she's learning in phase I to get it just right. Tracey is a perfectionist.

Perfectionism is the enemy of productivity. If you procrastinate, you are probably a perfectionist. If you tend to put off some tasks or projects, there is a high chance the reason is that you want to "do it right." Researchers have found that perfectionism results from one of three types of thinking: expecting perfect results from yourself, expecting perfect results from others, or thinking that others expect perfect results from you.

Being a productive leader is about creating a mindset that allows you to efficiently accomplish your work. It's about getting your work out the door so that you can get out of the office at a reasonable hour. In this chapter, we show you four evidence-based tools to make you even more productive: replace "just do it" with "just plan it"; trick yourself into getting started; set habits, not just goals; and work less to accomplish more.

1. REPLACE "JUST DO IT" WITH "JUST PLAN IT"

We all know the Nike mantra, "Just do it," and have come to believe that this is also the path to greater productivity. Wrong. Although "just do it" works in some situations, research shows that it should be replaced with "just plan it." Creating a brief plan before diving into your work actually improves productivity.

Two Days After Christmas

Psychologist Peter Gollwitzer of Columbia University wanted to learn what moves people to action. He recruited university students to participate in an experiment. Half the students were simply told to write a report about how they spent their Christmas Eve and send it in to the researchers by December 27. The other half were given the same assignment, but in addition, Gollwitzer asked them to identify exactly when and where they would write the report. Students picked a specific time (such as after breakfast) and a certain place (such as the quiet corner of the living room). In effect, these students had set what we call a *triggering event*. What happened? Seventy-one percent of the students who identified up front *when* and *where* they would write the report mailed it in by the due date. A meager 32 percent of the other group turned the report in on time. Gollwitzer's study has been replicated about 100 times in dozens of settings. The bottom line? You may be twice as likely to accomplish your work if you decide up front when and where you will do it.

Increase Your Odds

Often we are in roles in which we need something from one of our employees, peers, or business partners to get our own work done. Using the when-and-where research, a useful corollary is that it is easier to get people to do a task when you have set a triggering event in their heads or, better yet, when you have agreed with them on a particular when and where. For example, making a request such as, "Joe, could you bring me that report to the conference room after the 10 a.m. meeting?" is more likely to get you that report than is a general request such as "Joe, could you bring me that report tomorrow?"

What We Can Learn from Smokers

After studying 30,000 smokers who successfully kicked the habit, the psychologist James Prochaska developed a model for the ways people create change in their lives. One of his most significant findings is that people often rush into action ("I will stop smoking tomorrow") before they've set up the necessary groundwork for implementing that change (such as throwing away all their cigarettes). Intentions may be sincere, but without the proper planning, there is little chance of success. Therefore, before you rush to action, take time out and plan the day, week, or month ahead. Also, in planning your actions, set triggers for yourself.

2. TRICK YOURSELF INTO GETTING STARTED

In the Tom Cruise movie *Minority Report*, the PreCrime unit knows about a crime before it is committed. What if you could know what you're going to accomplish each day before you actually accomplish it?

Margaret did exactly that in writing this book. Nearly every Friday, she worked on a section of the book, and at the end of the workday, she sent Senia an email describing her progress and attached the latest version. But when did Margaret write the email to Senia? When she sat down at her computer, first thing in the morning. Even before working on the sections, she drafted the email—in the past tense—describing what she had completed that day. In a sense, Margaret was tricking herself into getting started. Here are two more techniques to trick yourself into getting started: use the Zeigarnik (pronounced Zay-gar-nick) effect and use Tina's ta-da! list.

The Zeigarnik Effect

Research that's almost 100 years old has been a bit of a productivity secret. The psychology researcher Bluma Zeigarnik discovered that *not* finishing a task in one sitting can be a good thing. Imagine that you agree to participate in a study in which a researcher gives you about 20 tasks to complete one by one (the tasks include making a clay figure, doing arithmetic, making a cardboard box, and completing puzzles). But while you are working on those tasks, he interrupts you on half of them before you have a chance to finish them (the order of interruptions was made to appear to be random). At the end of the study, the researcher asks you to tell him which tasks you worked on. Will you be more likely to remember the tasks you were working on when you were interrupted or the ones you had a chance to complete? Intriguingly, interrupted tasks are better remembered.

How can you apply this to your work? Leave a project only partly finished on your desk so that when you approach it the following morning, there's something to work on immediately. This is the *Zeigarnik effect*. Leave yourself loose ends: outlines before full paragraphs or draft presentations before the finished product.

One of our clients, Sanjay, was not a morning person. He often had a hard time getting started in the morning. He also hated wasting time. The Zeigarnik effect was just what he needed. Sanjay had decided to restructure his information technology department to better align it with the various lines of business his organization supported. "I've talked to all the key stakeholders," he told us, "but I need to send out an email announcing the changes before I hold my town hall meeting tomorrow afternoon." We asked, "What if you drafted the announcement this afternoon but waited to reread it one last time before hitting the send button in the morning? That way you would have something to do first thing when you arrive." Not only did Sanjay try this technique, but we later learned that he left something unfinished nearly every day so that he had something to jump-start his morning.

What's necessary for the Zeigarnik effect to work is to start something. For example, say you want to approach a potential client but are not sure how. The Zeigarnik effect does not work if you merely think, "I should approach this client." You need to start an action in order to leave some loose ends. Write out some bullet points for the way you will approach the client or do an Internet search to gather some information about the company. Then stop. Come back to it later and you'll be even more productive.

Will You Be More Likely to Wash Your Car for the First Time or the Third Time?

Another way to trick yourself into making progress is to pretend that you have already started. Two researchers ran a study at a professional car wash. After their first car wash, 300 customers received a free loyalty card. Half of those customers got a loyalty card with spaces for eight stamps. The deal was this: purchase eight car washes and get the next one free. The other half got a loyalty card with spaces for 10 stamps, but the first 2 stamps were already affixed (such that one-fifth of the card was already complete). Over the next nine months, the car wash tracked how many free washes were redeemed. In the eight-stamp group, 19 percent of the customers completed all eight stamps and received a free car wash. In the 10-stamp group with 2 stamps already affixed, 32 percent of the customers completed the remaining 8 stamps and received a free

car wash. People persisted more when the task had already been started for them.

How can you focus on being in progress on a project or task as opposed to being at the beginning of it? Try what we call Tina's ta-da! list trick. One of our clients, Tina, writes a couple of items on her to-do list that she has already accomplished and then immediately crosses them out. Ta-da! "Nothing feels better than seeing a couple of strikethroughs on my to-do list," she confesses. Sounds crazy? Maybe, but it works.

One Minute in Front of the TV

Julie is the pseudonym of a patient of Robert Maurer, a psychologist at UCLA. Julie was an overweight, overworked single mom with diabetes. Maurer knew that his typical advice (get 30 minutes of exercise per day) would probably not work for Julie. Instead he asked, "Do you watch TV?"

Julie looked at him quizzically and answered, "Yes."

"Could you stand up and walk for one minute while you watch TV?"

Julie looked at Maurer, wondering if he was making fun of her, and said, "Yes."

They agreed that for the next two weeks, each day while she watched TV, she would stand up and walk in place for only one minute. Julie came back two weeks later and enthusiastically reported, "What else can I do for one minute a day?" Maurer in a sense had tricked her into starting an exercise program. Over the next three months, Julie kept finding short periods of time to exercise. It wasn't so hard after all. In fact, one study shows that exercising in 5-minute increments throughout the day for a total of 30 minutes has the same physiological benefits as exercising for 30 minutes straight.

Let's transfer this thinking to the workplace. How can you trick yourself into starting a project on which you have been dragging your feet? From the outside looking in, Carla seemed like she wasn't able to consistently complete all her projects on time. But make no mistake: she was no slacker. It's that Carla rarely got to the more strategic projects her boss was looking for her to lead, and that was hurting her career. Instead, she spent her day dealing with the crisis du jour. She came to us at a low point.

"I feel like things are out of control," she said. "The faster I go, the behinder I get. I've got to make headway on this talent strategy, but I never have a chunk of time to work on it."

"What would you do if you had just five minutes to work on it?" we asked.

"I need way more time than five minutes," she countered, visibly annoyed that we would suggest such a lame idea.

"Sure you do, but what would you do if you had just five minutes?" we persisted.

"Probably jot down the people I need to get input from and set up a couple of meetings."

"Good. That's a start," we said. "What else could you do to move the project along by only 1 percent? Or put another way, what's the smallest step you could take that would have the biggest, most positive impact?"

"I guess I could pull up the template that's out on our company's intranet and start filling in what I already know," Carla offered.

"Now, that's a good start. When we talk next week, we will want you to brag about all the small steps you took to move this project forward."

Carla came to the next coaching call and shared the progress she had made on her talent strategy. She had tricked herself into taking tiny incremental steps on an important project.

GET GOING: QUESTIONS THAT MOVE PEOPLE TO ACTION

Ask these simple yet powerful questions to help yourself, your employees, and coworkers get a jump start on just about anything:

- What would you do if you had only five minutes?

- What could you do to move this project along by just 1 percent?

- What's the smallest step you could take that would have the biggest, most positive impact?

While these last two tools —just plan it and trick yourself into getting started—are about creating new behaviors to boost your productivity, our next tool is about stopping something altogether.

3. SET HABITS, NOT JUST GOALS

What do getting promoted, exercising daily, and writing a book have in common? They're all goals. What do smoking, nail biting, and interrupting others have in common? They're all habits. Ever since we were little kids, we've been told that goals are good and habits are bad. However, evidence shows that when it comes to being successful and productive, creating positive habits and routines can beat just setting goals.

What We Can Learn from Drug Addicts

Narcotics counselors will tell you that the chances of an addict quitting are quite slim. Addicts can only replace one habit, such as cocaine, with another habit, such as gum chewing. Why? Besides the obvious addictive nature of the drug of choice, there is something even more powerful going on: habits change the brain. One of the foremost researchers on this subject, Ann Graybiel of MIT, found that you cannot actually drop an old habit. Habits are deeply set inside the brain. However, you can create a new habit on top of an old one. Think of a habit as being like a well-worn path through the woods. Although you cannot make that path completely disappear, you can cut another path through the woods. Over time, with more use, that new path will become your brain's go-to response.

Psychologist Wendy Wood of the University of Southern California and her colleagues studied the ability of students to stick with a new, positive habit even when their circumstances change. Wood studied students who transferred midyear to a new college and who also had a strong exercise routine at their former school. The students for whom the circumstances or environment were very similar—same distance to the gym, similar class schedule to work around—reported that they stuck with their exercise habit. The students for whom the environment changed quite a bit were more likely to drop their exercise routine.

Wood and her colleagues point to the importance of frequency and environment in cultivating habits. Those students for whom the gym was in a similar environment—same distance from the new dorm—and whose class schedules were compatible with the same workout frequency adhered to their exercise regimen. It wasn't something they needed to think about. It didn't require additional mental energy. Using exercise as an example, this means that people who view exercise as a habit do so automatically—they don't even think about it.

"You wouldn't think of leaving the house without brushing your teeth, right?" says Mhayse Samalya, senior executive at Farmers, a leading U.S. property and casualty insurer. "Well, that's the same way I think about my morning workout. I don't even think about it. I just do it."

We can transfer this thinking to the workplace. One of our clients, Peter, works in the risk management area for a large commercial construction firm. One of his responsibilities is to be the go-to person on industry trends in his department. He sets a reminder on his calendar to do an Internet search every Friday between 3:30 and 5 p.m. rather than squeezing in shorter periods at random points during the week.

Deborah, a client who heads a call center for a claims-processing unit, has a goal of staying on top of her email. She creates a habit to check email four times a day for 10 minutes—8 a.m., 11 a.m., 2 p.m., and 6 p.m.—not whenever a new email pops up. Remember the real and hidden costs of flip-flopping.

Same Time, Same Place

Be aware that sometimes we need a short dose of conscious thought to move from a goal to a habit. For example, although you may intend to exercise on a business trip, you may not exercise as much or at all because you are away from your usual routine. The hotel gym is not the natural context for you. You will probably need to focus more conscious thought, such as remembering to pack your gym clothes and asking upon check-in for the location of the gym. But keep in mind that even hotel gym workouts can become a habit if they are repeated frequently enough.

One of our clients, Chris, had a goal to complete a redesign of his website by the end of the third quarter. However, as a business owner, he never seemed to find the time to focus on it while juggling dozens of other responsibilities. "So let's think about how often and where you will do this work," we said.

"It typically slows down around here between three and five on Fridays."

"Good," we said. "Now let's imagine where you'll actually work on this project. In your office, at home, or somewhere else?"

Chris replied, "I'll use the conference room at the end of the hall so that I'll be free from interruptions and not tempted by other distractions like the phone and email."

We checked in with Chris a month later. His new website was almost ready to go live, thanks to his new habit.

Outsource Yourself

Think about habits as outsourcing some of your work to the automatic part of your brain. Just as many companies outsource some of their repeatable processes to India or China, you can outsource some of your work too. Should you outsource everything to habits? No. Outsource only the more routine, less complex, and repeatable tasks.

Matthew runs a legal team at a law firm. His office was a disaster. Piles of manila folders from the last six months' worth of cases were stacked on the floor. It was driving him crazy. But even more important, his disorganized office led his colleagues and clients to think he was overwhelmed and not on top of his game. We told him about the power of habits and asked, "What if you applied the notion of habits to cleaning up your office?"

Matthew was skeptical. "Are you kidding? My office has always looked like this. You think I can break a 15-plus-year habit?"

"Sure. What if you set aside 10 minutes at the end of each day to organize your files?"

"Yeah, I guess I can try that," Matthew agreed.

Two weeks later, when we visited Matthew again, his desk was clear and the piles had vanished. In just 10 minutes a day, less than an hour a week, he had created a new clean-office habit. But the best part? Matthew felt more focused at work. He had decluttered his office, but more important, he had decluttered his mind.

4. WORK LESS, ACCOMPLISH MORE

Betsy is known for delivering results. From the time she arrives in the morning to the time she leaves in the evening, she spends her day putting out fires. Admirable? Yes. A way to advance her career? No. Besides burnout and friends and family who say, "Betsy who?" working more can be a career derailer. How? You can become known as a doer rather than a leader. What's wrong with that? Well, if all you do is put out fires, your manager will never get to see that you think strategically, that you can come up with ideas and plans to prevent fires from occurring in the first place. In fact, your manager may be afraid to promote you because your project or department will fall apart if he does. So guess what happens? You get passed over for promotions.

What Thoroughbred Horses and Boats Have in Common

Have you ever noticed that the owners of thoroughbred horses have the craziest names for their prized possessions, names like I'll Have Another, I Want Revenge, and Never Look Back? Boat owners do the same thing. Stroll down the dock of any marina and you're sure to find names like *Reel Time*, *Campbell's Sloop*, and *Aquaholic*. Margaret and her husband named their boat *Unplugged*. Some people ask if her husband is an electrician when they see the unplugged electrical cord painted on the stern of the boat. Others think *Unplugged* was chosen because he's an acoustic guitarist. The real origin of the name *Unplugged*? There is one rule on the boat: no work allowed! All electronics, with the exception of the navigational ones, must be left on shore. Yes, Margaret and her husband take their cell phones with them for emergencies, but checking email is taboo.

In our 24/7 world, where boundaries between work and the rest of life become blurred, people are finding it harder and harder to unplug, and their work is suffering as a result. Cases of insomnia, alcoholism, and caffeine addiction are increasing, and all can be linked to an increasingly stressful lifestyle. The previous three tools were about improving productivity within your current schedule and plans. This tool is about working less but accomplishing more.

Author of *Sleeping with Your Smartphone* and Harvard Business School professor Leslie Perlow conducted a four-year study and found that scheduling time off rather than working more hours actually boosted individual and organizational productivity. Perlow and her colleague Jessica Porter found in a survey of 1,000 professionals that 94 percent of them said they worked 50 or more hours a week and about half the respondents worked over 65 hours a week. That is not counting the 20 to 25 hours a week most respondents reported monitoring their smartphones while outside the office. In a drastic move, Perlow and Porter asked some groups in several North American offices of the Boston Consulting Group (BCG) to cut back work from five days a week to four. Perlow and Porter challenged the notion that consultants need to be available at all times. BCG was worried about how its clients would respond, and so they added an extra consultant to each four-person team. The consultants were required to take "predictable time off" and told that they couldn't even check email or voice mail at certain hours. The results? The BCG consultants streamlined their work and in fact accomplished as much or more in four days than they did in five. Communication between consultants improved, and some clients reported better customer service.

Sony Pictures Entertainment has figured out how to boost productivity by teaching employees how to avoid burnout. Sony has trained employees at all levels in ways to renew their energy by cultivating specific habits or rituals such as disconnecting from email during certain periods of the day to focus on an important project or task, taking a daily midafternoon walk, and going to the company gym during work hours. Eighty-eight percent of the employees who participated in the training believe it has made them more productive and focused, and 84 percent believe they are better able to manage the demands of their jobs. Although you cannot attribute company performance solely to this training, Sony's leaders believe it has contributed to their continued strong performance despite difficult economic conditions.

One summer, Senia worked for a large gas company in Tokyo. She spent a week with a branch office, shadowing employees in the office and as they visited customers' homes. What surprised Senia the most was not so much the mandatory one-hour lunch break as the way employees chose to spend the time. After a 10-minute meal in the cafeteria, employees played cards, took a nap, or meditated in the bamboo tatami resting room. They pointed to the after-lunch tatami-room practice as both energizing and relaxing and believed it made them more productive in the afternoon.

Avoiding Burnout One Yoga Room at a Time

Meditation has its roots in Eastern cultures and has made its way west with the introduction of yoga and meditation rooms in offices large and small across the country. Courses like Mindfulness Training now appear next to Finance 101 and Negotiation Skills in company learning and development curricula. Although they were first adopted by West Coast high-tech start-ups, these innovative offerings designed to help employees become more focused are being adopted by more mainstream corporations such as General Mills, Target, and Aetna.

Aetna's chairman and CEO Mark Bertolini practices daily meditation. He says, "Every morning I get up and I do my asana, pranayama, meditation and Vedic chanting before work." Bertolini has implemented an optional mindfulness and yoga program at Aetna, and over 3,500 employees have participated since 2010. The third largest health insurer now offers this program as part of its well-being service to help its customers lower healthcare costs. A mindful employee is not only a more productive employee but a healthier employee.

Our Vacation Policy: Yes

Amazon founder and CEO Jeff Bezos, Twitter founder Evan Williams, and Google chairman Eric Schmidt. What do these three technology giants have in common besides, well, technology? They all invested in EverFi, a DC-based education technology company dedicated to teaching students critical life skills such as financial planning and substance abuse prevention. What was so special about this company that it could attract the interest and financial backing of Bezos, Williams, and Schmidt?

Many companies now have in-house gyms and yoga studios and offer perks such as paid time off to help their employees unwind. But something unique we learned about EverFi is that it doesn't track paid time off the way most companies do. Unlimited paid vacation whenever you want as long as you tell your manager? We spoke with EverFi's cofounder and CEO Tom Davidson and learned that his philosophy on people shows up even in some mundane business practices such as his company's vacation policy.

"The most important asset that someone has is their time," said Davidson, recognized as one of the Top 100 Entrepreneurs of the Year by Goldman Sachs in 2012. "If you can't expect them to manage their time, then you really probably can't trust them with much else. At EverFi we have a clear vision and clear expectations, so I don't have to be in the plane ticket, vacation planning, and approval business."

We were skeptical, and so we probed a bit more. "Has there been any kind of abuse of this vacation policy?" we asked.

"We're north of a 100 employees now. I have yet to see it be abused. Ever. My whole MO is to try to create an atmosphere that unleashes people's creativity, and part of that is *not* to tell people when they can and can't go on vacation."

The Energizer Bunny

One of our clients, Cheryl, has a nickname among her staff members. They call her the Energizer Bunny. She goes and goes and goes and then collapses when she gets home from work. She has little energy left over for friends and family. She came to a coaching session desperate for advice. What Cheryl really needs is to give her brain a rest. She would actually be able to get more work done if she took a break at lunchtime and got away from her desk. However, Cheryl has been working through lunch her entire career. When we suggested that she start taking lunch breaks, Cheryl snapped: "Take a break? Are you kidding? There are barely enough hours in the day as it is."

"Okay, so what's the smallest change that you could make that would have the biggest impact?" we asked.

"I guess I could start by taking a lunch break on Fridays and go out for a walk now that the weather is nice."

"Okay, that's a good start. What else could you do?" Cheryl decided to turn off her smartphone when she gets home, at least for an hour or two. She had come up with two simple ways to give her brain a rest and allow her subconscious mind to process information and make new connections.

Consider how you can get yourself and your colleagues to stop overworking. Remember, it's hard to think in new and innovative ways when you're exhausted and stuck in old patterns.

KEY TAKEAWAYS

Two drains on our productivity are our own doing: we procrastinate and we multitask. But the other drain on our productivity is often externally driven: we're overworked. It used to be that the only way to work more was to be in the office. Today, thanks to technology, we can work anytime, anyplace. We all know people whose work becomes addictive and the rest of life becomes an interruption. Being productive is more than a collection of time management techniques. Being productive is a mindset that can be learned. Specifically, you can do the following:

- **Replace "just do it" with "just plan it."** Although you may have a bias for action that is highly valued, you'll be even more productive if you build in some time to plan your work. Carve out just 10 or 15 minutes at either the start or the end of the day to plan.

- **Trick yourself into getting started.** Sometimes we have to trick ourselves into thinking we've already started a project. We often procrastinate because the project seems overwhelming and inertia sets in. Think of a few steps you have already taken that will remind you that you're making headway.

- **Set habits, not just goals.** Although goals are worthwhile, you'll achieve them faster if you turn them into habits and routines. Remember: same time, same place.

- **Work less, accomplish more.** The productivity paradox is this: scheduling downtime actually makes you more productive. Don't be a prisoner chained to your desk. Get up and take periodic breaks. The solution to that knotty problem will become clearer when you give your brain a chance to process it.

Working longer and harder isn't going to make you more productive, but these tools will.

• • • REFLECTION QUESTIONS • • •

After reading this chapter, ask yourself these questions:

1. What am I already doing right when it comes to my own personal productivity?

2. When I procrastinate on a piece of work, how can I trick myself into thinking I've already started to propel me to action?

3. What's one goal I could turn into a habit?

4. How can I carve out some time each day for myself?

5. What is one small change I can make that will have the biggest, most positive impact on my productivity?

The Resilient Leader:
Give Yourself a Psychological Kick in the Pants

It's not enough to just be a productive leader. To get others to follow you, you also need to be a *resilient* leader. We all experience setbacks now and then in our careers such as losing a key customer account, flubbing a presentation to senior management, or being passed over for a promotion. But what matters most is how quickly we bounce back from negative events.

"If you want to be inventive, you have to be willing to fail," says Amazon founder and CEO Jeff Bezos. The world's largest online retailer has had its share of failures: hiring expensive editors to write book reviews and starting an auction business, among others. But unlike Bezos, most of us avoid failures like the plague, and when we do fail, we beat ourselves up and put ourselves under more and more stress.

Four O'Clock in the Morning

"I fall asleep fine," reports our client Richard, "but then I wake up around four in the morning and my mind is racing. I start making to-do lists in my head." Richard goes on to explain that minor hassles that he can solve by day transform themselves into enormous obstacles as he lies in bed waiting for the alarm to go off.

Richard is not alone. Not only do Americans report psychological and physical harm from stress, but the same is true around the world. A 2012 global study of over 16,000 employees found that stress at work increased by about 50 percent from the previous year. Of the countries studied, China (75 percent) and Germany (58 percent) had the highest spikes in stress. Additionally, employees who work for a larger company tend to be about twice as likely to feel stressed.

We tend to view stress as an *external* event, such as losing a job or trying to make ends meet in a poor economy. What we don't realize sometimes is that stress is *our reaction* to external events; stress is not the event itself. The good news is that we can train ourselves to respond to stressful events in a healthier way.

In coaching hundreds of business owners and executives, we've found two common but counterproductive responses to negative events: we ruminate, and we become paralyzed.

We ruminate. "How did your presentation to the executive committee go last week?" we asked Laura, who leads a quality assurance function for a Fortune 200 company.

"Okay, I guess," she replied halfheartedly. "But I'm so mad at myself for getting tripped up on one of the questions the sponsor asked me. I blabbed on and on when I should have just said, 'I'll look into that and get back to you.'"

"How many other questions did you field?" we asked. Laura thought for a moment.

"Oh, I don't know; probably a dozen or so," she replied.

We got curious. "And would you say you handled those other questions well?" Laura smiled. Our one simple question had produced an aha moment. She realized that she had been replaying that one mistake over and over in her mind for the better part of a week. She had become a master of playing the second-guessing game and was losing every hand.

We become paralyzed. A decade ago, Senia cofounded a start-up company. The start-up was developing a technology prototype for a large consumer goods company.

"The brand manager was helpful," Senia recalls. "He was keen on the project and gave us the right amount of autonomy. We delivered a strong prototype and were in discussions to work together on a large project. One day he called to inform us that he was about to be transferred to another office. Additionally, he said that he had run our large project by his successor and, 'It's not a priority for him.'"

This was a fairly large disappointment to Senia, her cofounder, and the rest of the team. She began diagnosing what went wrong.

"I started thinking, should I have built more support for the project by getting the brand manager's boss involved earlier in the process? In short, when our contact left, our project came to a complete halt. Rather than brainstorming ways we could move this project forward, we kept looking backward."

Sometimes when we experience similar setbacks, we get stuck and are unable to take action. This paralysis results in tunnel vision, both figuratively in terms of being less creative and literally in terms of having a narrower focus.

PTSD or Post-Traumatic Growth?

Psychologists now know that survivors of war and other atrocities can actually grow or develop from such negative events. This may sound counterintuitive at first. It could also make us think of Nietzsche's expression "That which does not kill us makes us stronger." Unfortunately, stories about people suffering from post-traumatic stress disorder (PTSD) tend to get more of the media's attention than do stories about people who grow from traumatic events. Positive psychology researchers study the other side of the traumatic coin, what's referred to as *post-traumatic growth*: the positive changes people often claim to experience in the months and years after a harrowing event. Researchers measure the positive change by asking people after a traumatic event the degree to which they agree with statements such as the following: "I discovered that I'm stronger than I thought I was," and, "I'm able to do better things with my life."

Researchers who study resilience, grit, and perseverance find that tough times can actually bring out the best in people. If anyone knows about traumatic events, it's the first responders who show up on the scene, such as firefighters, police officers, and emergency medical technicians. For example, in a study of emergency ambulance personnel, almost all the workers reported experiencing a traumatic event on the job within their first 18 months of employment. At the same time, over 95 percent of the workers reported experiencing at least a small positive change after the traumatic event.

Additionally, you are probably familiar with the nonprofit organization Mothers Against Drunk Driving, which was founded by a mom who lost her daughter to a drunk driver. Another example of post-traumatic growth is the case of Jill Bolte Taylor, a brain researcher who suffered a massive stroke and then used the insights she gained while recuperating to help others.

It is exactly when we're feeling stress, fear, and incompetence that we most need resilience. It is when we are at our lowest that we need some tools and techniques that can help us get unstuck. Sometimes we need to give ourselves a psychological kick in the pants. In this chapter, you will learn how to change not what you *do* but how you *think*. The three tools, as demonstrated in hundreds of studies, are to quit being an expert, put on an explorer's hat, and win debates against yourself.

1. DON'T QUIT, JUST QUIT BEING AN EXPERT

Chip Conley is the founder of Joie de Vivre Hotels. He started the company at age 26 when he bought his first motel in the San Francisco Bay area, and over the last 25 years he has increased the number of eclectic hotels to nearly 40. However, Joie de Vivre was hit hard by the dot-com bust of 2002, when travelers to the Bay Area declined.

How did a hotel chain named "the joy of living" survive the bust and go on to be California's largest boutique hotel collection? We asked Conley. "One of the qualities that I think undergirds or fuels resilience is curiosity," he told us. "And quite often the epiphanies in life come when there is a fertilizer going on between what you already know and disparate elements in the world that help you see things in a new way."

For Conley, the epiphany came when he visited a bookstore during the company's darkest times. Rather than being drawn to the business section, he was drawn to a book in the self-help section on Maslow's hierarchy of needs. This book became Joie de Vivre's "constitution for how we got through the downturn, and not only got through it, but tripled in size," he told us. Curiosity was the key.

For decades, Stanford psychologist Carol Dweck has been studying how people in situations like Conley's face challenges. Dweck found that when given a difficult task, some people get excited about the challenge and work harder, whereas others become withdrawn and give up quickly. Even more interesting is that Dweck and other researchers could induce the excited-about-the-challenge mindset in a lab setting, which means this mindset is not only innate but can also be learned. All it took to change the way people approach a challenge was to tell them what kind of task they were about to perform: a task that would demonstrate how capable they were or one that would show them how much they would learn.

The experimenter told the participants, "In this box we have problems of different levels to solve. Some are hard, some are easier. If you pick this box, although you won't learn new things, it will really show me what you can do." Unknowingly, the participants had been offered a *performance task*.

"If you pick the tasks in this other box," the researcher went on to explain, "you'll probably learn a lot of new things. But you'll probably make a bunch of mistakes, get a little confused, maybe feel a little dumb at times—but you'll learn some useful things." These participants had been offered a *learning task*.

As in any good research study, there was a twist. The content of the two boxes was identical. However, this simple manipulation in the way the task was described influenced whether a participant took on the challenge or avoided the challenge altogether. Additionally, some participants were told that they would be filmed and evaluated by a group of experts (performance task), and others were told that the tasks would "sharpen the mind" (learning task). Among those who were told they would be filmed, only 66 percent chose the task ("it will really show me what you can do"). Among those who were told this would sharpen their minds, 82 percent chose the task ("you'll probably learn a lot of new things"). Thus, if participants were told they would be evaluated, they wanted to show off their skills, and if they were told it would sharpen their minds, they wanted to learn more.

The So-What Factor

When people have a *learning mindset,* they tend to focus more on effort and gaining competence. When people have a *performance* or *expert mindset,* they tend to focus more on their ability and demonstrating their competence. You might be thinking, so what? People with a performance mindset believe they either have the ability or they don't. This mindset determines if they will even take on a challenging assignment, and if they do, how much of a failure they feel when they make mistakes and how likely they are to give up. People with a learning mindset, however, believe they can always put in more effort and improve with less fear of failure. They are less likely to give up or quit a challenging assignment.

If you are a manager and are responsible for distributing new and challenging assignments to your team, frame the work as an opportunity to learn the way we coached our client Rosanna to do.

Rosanna runs the program office at a medium-sized technology company. She had a highly visible project she wanted to give to one of her employees, Jonathan, whom she was grooming to be her successor. Although it would be a stretch assignment, it would give him exposure to her company's management team and the field. In her next one-on-one with Jonathan she positioned the new assignment.

"I'd like to give you the opportunity to lead our next release," Rosanna began. "There are a lot of unknowns at this point, but I'm confident we can figure this out together. What do you hope to learn from this assignment?"

"I really hope I gain a better understanding for how the field interfaces with the home office," Jonathan replied. "I also hope I

BE A LEARNER: QUESTIONS THAT BOOST PERFORMANCE AND REDUCE FEAR

The next time you or someone you work with is about to start a challenging new assignment, try these coaching questions to promote a learning mindset:

- How can your past experiences help you with this current challenge?

- What do you hope to learn from this new project?

- What are some mistakes you might make? And what would you say to persuade yourself that it's okay to make mistakes like these once in a while?

can learn more about our legacy systems so we can figure out a strategy to sunset them."

"That sounds good," Rosanna replied. "I want you to know that no release is perfect and you'll probably make some mistakes along the way, but I am here to support you."

A learning mindset builds our competency and resilience. When we frame new assignments as an opportunity to learn, employees are more enthusiastic and willing to put in the extra effort to complete them.

Mistake-of-the-Month Club

One of the practical ways in which Chip Conley encouraged a learning mindset at Joie de Vivre Hotels was his Mistake-of-the-Month club. Once a month, someone at the company would get an award for "a mistake they made that helped them have some new learning or wisdom that far exceeded the cost," Conley told us. What an excellent way to benefit from a learning mindset.

We started this chapter by telling you about Amazon's founder. Bezos believes that a desire to invent and explore—what we call a learning mindset—is necessary at all levels of the company and is key to Amazon's goal to be "the world's most customer-centric company." Bezos says that, "You have to have a willingness to fail, to be misunderstood for long periods of time. . . . Successful invention requires you to increase your rate of experimentation."

When we quit trying to be an expert and instead become more of a *learner*, we are better able to face challenging situations. We are more resilient, and that can lead to more innovation. But how can we be creative when we may believe that we have few options? Read on.

2. PUT ON AN EXPLORER'S HAT

Our mentor Martin Seligman is the author of *Learned Optimism*, in which he describes his research on how people differ in explaining the same event. He argues that optimism is not a glass-half-full, la-la-land perspective and that it can be summarized as simply the words we use to explain good and bad events. He calls this *explanatory style*. In this tool, we examine the explorer's hat we can all wear to discover the explanatory style we want to use in specific situations.

Explanatory style can be broken into three distinct components: personal (did I cause this event?), permanent (is this event changeable?), and pervasive (does this event affect other parts of my life?). In *The Resilience Factor*, Karen Reivich and Andrew Shatté offer a simple framework to describe explanatory style: Me-Always-Everything.

THE ME-ALWAYS-EVERYTHING FRAMEWORK

When a bad event occurs, ask yourself the following questions:

- *Me:* Did I cause this? Or did external events cause this? Or a combination of both?

- *Always:* Does this kind of situation always happen to me? Or is this a one-off setback and changeable?

- *Everything:* Is this event going to spill over into other domains in my life? Or is this an isolated situation?

For example, if a salesperson with an *optimistic explanatory* style fails to close a big account, he will most likely think in terms of **Not** Me ("Maybe I wasn't on top of my game, but there were circumstances beyond my control"), **Not** Always ("So I didn't close one big account? That doesn't mean I won't later this month"), and **Not** Everything ("Okay, so I didn't make the sale, but I'm still a good husband and father").

When we apply this same Me-Always-Everything thinking to a *positive* event, just the opposite is true for someone with an optimistic explanatory style. Imagine that the same salesperson closes five big sales, all in one day. He will mostly likely think in terms of Me ("I caused this cascade of strong sales"), Always ("These wins tend to happen to me all the time"), and Everything ("I'm on a roll; good things seem to be happening everywhere in my life").

Why use the Me-Always-Everything framework as a way to structure your thinking when things go bad? Because when bad events happen, it's easy to go into a downward ruminative spiral of, "Why does this always happen to me?" Counteract this spiral with opposing thoughts: for a bad event, consider how it might be "Not Me–Not Always–Not Everything." In contrast, for good events, to simulate an optimistic explanatory style, go ahead and cheer for yourself. A good thing happened? Well, it must be "Me–Always–Everything."

When things go right or wrong, you can put on your explorer's hat to uncover more empowering perspectives that may not come naturally to you. What is the probability that everything will go wrong? Usually not 100 percent.

CHANGE YOUR PERSPECTIVE BY CHANGING YOUR QUESTIONS

From our experience in coaching hundreds of clients, here are a half dozen perspectives you can try on to help shift a negative, explanatory style into a more positive one:

- **The future perspective.** What would you say about this 20 years from now?

- **The past perspective**. Looking back, when have you conquered a similar situation?

- **The severity perspective**. How bad is this compared with other situations you've faced?

- **The distance perspective.** How would this look from 30,000 feet in the air? What's the bigger picture here?

- **The extremes perspective**. What is the worst thing that could possibly happen? What's the best thing that could possibly happen? And then, really, what is the most *likely* thing that will happen?

- **The best friend perspective.** What would your best friend advise you to do?

One of our colleagues, Bob, didn't get the promotion he was hoping for. He had been in the running with three other internal candidates for the regional head job. He thought he had all the experience the talent review board was looking for and had aced the group interview. When he didn't get the promotion, he began to doubt his abilities and came to us for some advice.

"I'm really disappointed," Bob confessed. "I'm not sure what I should do next."

"Before you ask your boss if there is anything you could have done differently to get the regional head position, you need to bounce back from this disappointment," we offered. "If you're ever going to be considered for other promotions, you need to demonstrate that you're a resilient leader. Let's put on your explorer's hat and try on some other perspectives. What would you say about this 20 years from now?"

Bob smiled. "That Bob would probably say, 'What regional head job?'"

"What else would he say?"

"He'd probably say, 'Okay, so you didn't get this job, but there were other opportunities that came along.'"

The goal in exploring other perspectives is to create flexibility in our thinking. It is not to create an excuse for what may have actually gone wrong. Instead, considering other perspectives can minimize the impact of a negative event and spur us to action. When we reframe the way we view a setback or negative event, often it starts to appear less overwhelming. Neutralize its negative power by trying on other, more positive perspectives.

Nido Qubein knows a thing or two about being resilient. He lost his father at age 6 and came to America at age 17 with only $50 in his pocket. Today he is the chairman of Great Harvest Bread Company, a chain of 230 bakeries in the United States; president of High Point University in North Carolina; and a board member for two New York Stock Exchange companies. Equipping people with life skills such as resilience is so important to him that as busy as he is, he finds the time to teach a mandatory course for all incoming freshman called the President's Seminar on Life Skills. When times are tough or things go wrong, he told us, "It's okay to get disappointed, but it's not okay to get discouraged. When in doubt, look backwards." What Qubein means is that you have probably had other setbacks in your life and you survived. "To me, resilience means you have the faith and confidence in yourself, and that is based on competence and courage. Positive thinking alone doesn't do the job."

Sleeping with the Enemy

Being a resilient leader can be learned, but sometimes we are our own worst enemy. We engage in conversations with ourselves that are anything but empowering. In this last tool, learn how to stop your sabotaging self-talk in its tracks.

3. WIN DEBATES AGAINST YOURSELF

Sometimes our current situation may seem daunting. But if we take a moment to reflect, we may find that we have faced and overcome other challenges in the past. We have the proof. We have the *evidence*. By focusing on evidence—a particular time when we conquered a setback or achieved something that seemed unimaginable—we can load up our defenses and ready ourselves to tackle the current setback. Psychologists call this evidence-building technique *disputing*.

Disputing is the cornerstone of a powerful area of study that preceded positive psychology called *cognitive behavioral therapy* (CBT). It works like this. Together a client and a therapist examine a particularly challenging or adverse event and the client's reaction to it; for example, what thoughts are going through his mind in response to his divorce. In other words, what is his self-talk? If the self-talk is negative, such as, "I'm a complete failure," the therapist helps the person find evidence from his past to dispute his negative beliefs. The therapist may ask, "Describe for me a time in your life when you succeeded at something." CBT is a highly effective tool for eliminating psychological issues, including panic attacks. If CBT can help people with something as severe as panic attacks, imagine what it can do when applied to everyday work issues.

For example, after pounding the pavement for nine hours and not making a single sale, a salesperson may be thinking, "I made 20 cold calls today without even a hint of a sale. This is going to be a terrible week. What's the matter with me? I'm not cut out for this. I guess I'm not good with people or very persuasive."

With beliefs like this, you can probably imagine how successful this salesperson will be the rest of the week. However, he has a choice. He can go into a downward spiral or he can dispute these negative beliefs. Disputing is a technique that builds resilience by not viewing setbacks as a personal flaw that affects all aspects of our lives but instead viewing them as a temporary blip on the radar screen. Let's replay the above scenario with a salesperson who uses the disputing technique.

"Okay, so I'm not doing a very good job, but I'm new at this. My boss said she struggled for the first couple of months too, learning the tools of the trade and building her network and client base. A couple of coworkers who went through the training with me have shared similar experiences. I remember feeling incompetent early on in my last job, and I ended up being one of the top performers. It takes lots of hard work and practice to get good at any skill, and sales is no exception."

Notice the difference between the two responses to the same event. In the second scenario the salesperson is disputing the negative beliefs that pop into his head with actual evidence from not only his past experience but also from his boss's and colleagues' experience. Unlike the salesperson in the first scenario, this sales rep will have the fortitude to get back out on the road and make more cold calls, which will likely turn into some sales.

One of our clients, Carol, runs an operation that has been hit hard by the economy. Sales are off, and the company doesn't need as many service reps processing orders as it used to. She came to one of her coaching calls and didn't sound like her normal upbeat self. We soon learned why.

"I had to lay off five people yesterday. I hate doing this. I'm sure my staff thinks I'm a bad manager. Maybe I am." Carol had been debating with herself the better part of a day, and she was losing.

If you're like many leaders we know, you have faced a similar situation. The day layoffs don't make you feel lousy is the day you have lost your humanity. Telling someone he no longer has a job is difficult. But how can you move forward and continue to lead the rest of your team? Let's see what we can learn from Carol's story.

"Okay, so you think you're a bad manager," we replied. "Let's dispute your negative self-talk by providing some evidence to the contrary. Begin by filling in the blank: 'I'm not a bad manager because....'"

Carol was hesitant at first. "I'm not a bad manager because ... I know my employees feel valued."

We urged Carol on. "Okay, good. Provide some more evidence for why you're not a bad manager."

"Our company has been hit hard, and in order to save 100 jobs, I had to lay off these five employees. If we don't remain competitive, all of our work will be outsourced."

Carol was starting to win the debate against herself. We had helped her replace the self-defeating chatter inside her head with evidence to the contrary. You can do the same thing.

Carving a Boomerang for Others

You may be pretty good at bouncing back from disappointments, but if you're like many of our clients, you could use some advice on how to help your team. Rather than managing or controlling your employees, try coaching them instead. Let's put the three tools from this chapter together and see how they work.

For the last month, one of Carol's sales reps has been experiencing a lot of nos. In the last week alone, seven prospects have told Sergio that they're not interested in the product right now. They don't have the budget. Sergio is feeling like a failure and is dreading going out on the road. Carol is concerned that Sergio may quit. She asks Sergio questions that promote a *learning mindset*. "Sergio, let's see what we can learn from these declines that will help us tailor your next sales pitches."

Carol then coaches Sergio to *put on his explorer's hat* and try different perspectives: "Okay, these seven prospects are sunk costs, but this isn't going to put us out of business. For many companies, their budget cycle is about to start. What else can we do to bring in more business?"

Finally, Carol *provides evidence* that Sergio is not a lousy sales rep: "Sergio, you're one of our best sales reps. You've hit your numbers again and again and even exceeded them several times over the last year. You're just experiencing a rough patch right now— welcome to sales."

KEY TAKEAWAYS

We all experience setbacks now and then. That's life. But it's how quickly we bounce back from disappointments and adverse events that determines how successful, happy, and fulfilled we will be. How quickly a person bounces back is also what separates an average leader from a great one. It's not so much what you *do* but how you *think* that really matters. Rather than ruminating over a bad event or shying away from big challenges for fear of failure, try these three responses to build your resilience:

- **Don't quit, just quit being an expert.** Focus on what you can learn from your next challenge. When we reframe challenging assignments as opportunities to learn, this increases our effort.

- **Put on an explorer's hat.** The way a situation looks at first may not necessarily be an accurate view of reality, especially when we have a lens of fear, stress, or uncertainty. Try on other perspectives to expand your view.

- **Win debates against yourself.** When faced with a daunting situation, remember that you've overcome other obstacles in the past. Replace the negative self-chatter with evidence to the contrary.

Remember, we are not advocating that you pretend problems or setbacks don't exist. It's important that we take responsibility for the situations in which we find ourselves. But we are advocating that you change your self-talk. Practice using these methods on both yourself and your employees. Notice how your self-talk becomes more empowering and how much more quickly you bounce back from disappointments. These three tools will give you the psychological kick in the pants we all need now and then. Remember, your employees are counting on you.

● ● ● **REFLECTION QUESTIONS** ● ● ●

After reading this chapter, ask yourself these questions:

1. What am I already doing right to be a resilient leader?

2. When would taking on a learning mindset serve me or members of my team well?

3. Which one of my employees is having difficulty bouncing back from a failure or negative event, and how can I help him?

4. What's a negative belief I hold about myself ("I'm not good at . . .") that is just not true? What's the evidence to the contrary?

5. What is one small change I can make that will make me even more resilient?

THE CONTAGIOUS LEADER:
Control Your Emotions, Not Your Employees

George arrives at the office at 7:45 sharp every day. Two of his employees, Rachel and Mike, like to get in at around 7:15 so that they can grab a cup of coffee, catch up on emails, and get ready for the day ahead. Every morning they look up from their desks as George walks in. Rachel and Mike have an inside joke:

"We can tell what kind of day it's going to be around here by the way George walks in each morning. If he smiles and says, 'Good morning,' we know it's going to be a good day and we can get on with our work. If his head is down and he doesn't even acknowledge us, we know it's going to be a bad day and we'd better be ready to jump at a moment's notice. When our teammates arrive at around eight, they stop by our desks and ask us, 'So what kind of day is it going to be?' and believe me, they're not talking about the weather."

Unfortunately, you may have worked for a toxic boss like George at some point in your career. He may have humiliated you in front of others, micromanaged you to death, ranted and raved when things went wrong, or been a Scrooge who took all the fun out of work.

Chances are that you no longer work for him because you couldn't stand it any longer and transferred to another department or found another job. If you see a little of yourself in George or if he reminds you of someone you know, read on.

Toxic or abrasive bosses like George are often tolerated for much too long for three reasons: we overvalue technical competence and short-term results, we underestimate the negative effect, and we are afraid to speak up.

We overvalue technical competence. Many company decision makers overvalue the boss's technical competence and believe he is indispensable. We call this the "but she's really bright" syndrome. Although technical competence is important, we often undervalue emotional competence. In a study of 358 managers at Johnson & Johnson, researchers found that the managers who had the highest performance had significantly more emotional competence such as self-awareness, self-management, and social skills.

We underestimate the negative effect. The toxic boss's boss and sometimes even the human resources department are unaware, choose to ignore, or underestimate the negative effect he has on employees. Frequent resignations within the same department are viewed as isolated incidents. As long as the toxic boss continues to achieve results, regardless of his methods, he is left alone.

We are afraid to speak up. Toxic bosses are masters of creating an environment of fear in which workers don't dare to speak up. Imagine if the toxic boss is also the owner of the company. An employee may think her only option is to quit.

In this chapter, we offer an alternative to the toxic boss. We call it the *contagious leader*. We'll share evidence on how your moods, good or bad, affect your employees' productivity. You'll learn simple, proven techniques to neutralize a negative mood if you need to do that. We'll also show you how to manage the control freak tendencies that many of us have that can get in the way of not only your own productivity but also that of your team.

1. RECOGNIZE THE ACHOO! EFFECT

Germs and colds aren't the only things we spread in the workplace. Our emotions, both positive and negative, are just as contagious. Have you ever walked into an office or a meeting and felt so much tension that you became tense too? This spreading of emotions from one person to another is what psychologists call social contagion. We call it the *Achoo! effect*. Here's how it works.

Human beings are hardwired to mimic the facial expressions and moods of the people they come in contact with. Sigal Barsade, a professor at the Wharton School of Business at the University of Pennsylvania, claims that we can unconsciously catch both good and bad moods. Barsade studied this ripple effect and found that it takes only one group member out of five to "infect" the rest of the group with a positive or negative mood. Similarly, it has been found that bank tellers in a positive mood can transmit these emotions to their customers, which leads to greater customer satisfaction.

In another study, researchers observed over 200 customer service interactions at a coffee shop. What did they learn? The degree to which the employee smiled predicted the degree to which the customer smiled (above and beyond the customer's disposition when he or she entered the shop). When customers later rated their satisfaction with the service they received, the more employees smiled, the higher the rating was. In fact, neuroscientists point to "mirror neurons" in our brains that are wired to mimic other people's facial expressions. Ever notice that when you smile at an infant, the infant will smile back? The same is true for adults.

Bosses Are More Contagious

This Achoo! effect also has a status component: people higher up the ladder are more likely to transmit their moods to those lower in the company than vice versa. Think of it this way: when you're in a bad mood, it's like spreading a cold. When you have a cold or flu you feel lousy, and your productivity suffers as a result. The good news? Your positive moods are just as contagious. Think infectious like laughter. Think a YouTube video that has gone viral.

Researchers have also found that a leader's positive or negative mood can spread in as little as seven minutes and can impact a team's performance. In one study, teams were told that they would have 15 minutes to set up a tent while blindfolded. Separately, the leaders were given instructions on how to assemble the tent and then watched a video. Some leaders watched a David Letterman video to put them into a positive mood, while others watched a video about social injustice to instigate a negative mood. What happened? Even though the team couldn't see the leader while he was giving instructions, they caught the leader's mood (positive or negative). Secondly, observers reported that the teams led by the "positive mood" leaders exhibited a higher degree of coordination.

Okay, so moods are contagious. So what? The degree of co-ordination in assembling a tent is one thing, but what about performance in the workplace? In a study of 53 sales managers who led teams of four to nine people, leaders in more positive moods had greater sales.

Unfortunately, the reverse is true when the boss is in a foul mood: bad moods are just as contagious. Cindi Bigelow, president of Bigelow Tea, sums it up this way: "Leaders cannot afford the luxury of a negative mood." Bigelow acknowledges that leaders must get results and move the company forward but emphasizes that what matters is *how* it's done. She says, "When you are sincere . . . , you will get so much more from people. . . . You've got to admit when you make a mistake. You've got to admit when you need somebody's help. And you have to admit what you don't know. Then when you're true to yourself, [other people are] going to be there for you. . . ."

Our client David shared with us the anonymous feedback he received from one direct report in a 360-degree review. The employee's feedback practically mirrored Bigelow's comment about a leader's positive demeanor: "David has a passion and believes in what we do. That passion is contagious, and we all come to work feeling good about what we're doing. This is an invaluable quality."

The 411 on Delivering Bad News

As business leaders, we sometimes have difficult messages to deliver, such as poor quarterly results, the loss of a key account, layoffs, or unexpected delays in a project. These discussions can often be energy-draining just when we need people's creative juices to flow. What's a leader to do?

When you have bad news, aggregate it before you deliver it and deliver it like ripping off a Band-Aid. How do you feel when you lose something such as your house key? Pretty bad, right? How do you feel when you find something such as an extra key to the house? Okay, but researchers have found that the good is often not as strong as the bad. What is happening is that you are swayed—as are we all—by prospect theory.

Prospect theory is an intriguing behavioral economics concept that states that losses are more painful than gains are enjoyable. For this reason, if you have good news, spread it out over a day or a week, but if you have bad news, aggregate it all at once so that it is not as painful to hear: separate gains and aggregate losses.

Jason Fried, CEO of 37signals, is well aware of this dynamic. 37signals is an innovative company that creates software tools for individuals and small businesses. Fried says, "A side note about delivering news, bad and good: When bad news comes, get it all out in the open at once. Good news, on the other hand, should be trickled out slowly. If you can prolong the good vibes, do it."

2. TAME YOUR OSCAR THE GROUCH IF YOU NEED TO

After reading the previous section, you may be thinking that we are expecting you to be in a good mood no matter what comes your way. We are not. We're all too familiar with the downsides of business: laying off good workers, losing a big account, missing an important deadline. Bad things happen, and we wouldn't be human if we didn't feel disappointed, angry, or frustrated at times.

Unfortunately, most of us were never trained in how to quickly get out of a bad mood. If you played high school or college sports, maybe you were lucky enough to have a coach who instructed you to "shake it off." Or maybe you had a mom who told you, "This, too, shall pass." But we'd be surprised if you told us you learned how to manage your moods as part of a leadership or manager training curriculum. Instead, you probably learned how to improve employee productivity by analyzing performance metrics. Surprisingly, researchers are now finding that productivity may be related to the number of scowls and smiles.

What MRIs, Deep Breathing, Getting off Your Tush, and Faking It Have in Common

There are four demonstrated techniques to get yourself out of a negative mood, and none of them requires a lot of time or money. The first is to *label it.*

If you've ever had to slide yourself into an MRI (magnetic resonance imaging) machine, you know what stress can do to your body. Although the procedure is said to be painless, being strapped inside a sewerlike tunnel surrounded by a deafening thump, thump, thumping is anything but painless. Remaining completely still for a few seconds or minutes can seem like eons. But the burgeoning field of neuroscience has found that when patients tell the technician how they are feeling, saying things such as, "I'm anxious," the negative emotion dissipates more quickly than it does if they keep these feelings to themselves. The next time you find yourself in a lousy mood, try labeling it and notice what happens. The very act of naming what you are experiencing can minimize the negative emotion.

Another way to get out of a bad mood is to *take long, deep breaths*. Researchers have found that slow rhythmic breathing produces an immediate calming effect, allowing you to recover more quickly from everyday stressors.

Still another way to shrug off that negative mood is to *get off your tush*. When we're stuck in a negative mental state, the worst thing we can do is just sit at our desks or take it out on the next person who walks into our office. We often go on a "walk and talk" with our clients to help them let off steam, which then allows them to focus on what's really important. Notice what happens when you get up from your desk and walk around your office or down the halls of your building. If you can get outside, even better. Being in nature has also been found to reduce stress.

When all else fails, do what psychologists call embodiment. We call it *fake it till you make it*. Embodiment entails putting your *physical* body into a stance that then changes your *psychological* state. For example, standing with your shoulders back, your head up, and your legs firmly planted hip distance apart has been shown to make you feel more powerful. One of the most famous and earliest studies of embodiment is the pen smile study. Researchers told two groups of participants to hold a pen in their mouths under the guise that they were studying motor coordination. One group was instructed to hold the pen between their *teeth*. This pose is similar to the position our mouths take when we are smiling. The other group was told to hold the pen with their *lips* instead of their teeth. In this pose it was impossible for the participants to smile. (A third group was told to hold the pen in the nondominant hand).

While holding the pen, all three groups of participants read four *The Far Side* cartoons and then were asked to rate how funny they were. Those holding the pen with their teeth (and inadvertently

activating the smiling muscles) reported the cartoons as being funnier than did the ones holding a pen in their nondominant hand,
who in turn reported the cartoons as funnier than those who
couldn't smile because they were holding the pen with their lips.
Mothers everywhere will be glad to know there's some science now
behind their sage advice to "put on a happy face."

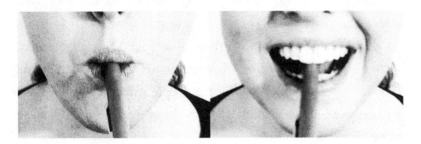

Pen Smile Study: Lips Holding Pen and Teeth Holding Pen

Sometimes you need to fake it until you make it. You can put
your body into a strong posture and smile *before* you feel like it.
These simple physical manipulations can actually get you out of
a funk and into a more positive mental state. And if you want to
snap someone else out of a foul mood, let's not forget the power
of humor. As our University of Pennsylvania classmate and come-
dian Yakov Smirnoff recently told us, "I think it's common sense
more than science. If you can make someone laugh, it releases the
tension."

Just Notice

Before you walk into work, notice what kind of mood you're in.
If you're in a good mood, great. Go ahead and spread the cheer.
But there are times when you may be feeling nervous, annoyed, or

impatient like our client George whom you met at the beginning of this chapter.

George's wife had recently lost her job when we met him. His mind was racing: "How will my wife find another job in this economy? How will we pay for our son's college tuition? How can we possibly live on one income?" George was feeling anxious, angry, and afraid—all very understandable under the circumstances.

But George also leads a team of people. We explained the Achoo! effect and told him that he cannot afford to let his foul mood affect the productivity of the people around him. George is a smart guy. He got it and began practicing the four techniques to tame his Oscar the Grouch.

However, a few weeks later, George came to a coaching call somewhat exasperated. "Sometimes getting yourself out of a negative mood seems impossible," he said.

George went on to explain that the day before, he had had a terrible meeting with his boss. His boss laid into him about the poor quarterly call with investors. George had five minutes before the start of his weekly staff meeting.

"I tried taking a few long, deep breaths on my way to the conference room, but I couldn't shake my lousy mood." George went on to explain that as he entered the conference room, he noticed that the friendly banter ended abruptly. "I guess my team could read my body language. They knew something was up and it wasn't good. They probably thought I was about to announce layoffs or something."

"So it sounds like everyone in the conference room was on edge. It seems they caught your mood, George. What did you do then?" we asked.

"I decided to be up front. I told the team I was feeling a bit distracted, but if we dove into the agenda, it would probably help me get back on track. And guess what? It did." George had labeled his emotion without even thinking about it.

Negative moods are inevitable, but successful leaders know how to get out of them quickly so that they don't negatively affect their employees' productivity or their own. Now that you know what to do, there's only one thing you must *not* do to be a positive, contagious leader: Don't be a control freak!

3. DON'T BE A CONTROL FREAK

One of our clients, Sarah, who heads a new provider network, landed a really big account. We wanted to know how she explained her success. "Do you believe your success is due to your hard work and perseverance?" we asked. "Or do you believe you signed this big account because the economy turned around?"

"Oh, my team and I worked really hard over the last three months to get this account. And right before our last client presentation, do you know what we did? We role-played every imaginable objection we could think of," Sarah replied. "We are definitely positioned to come out on top this quarter." This was her belief.

Psychologists can code such beliefs by their *locus of control*. Sarah has a strong *internal* locus of control. She believes she directly contributed to landing the big account and believes she can shape future outcomes. If Sarah had attributed landing the big account to the improved economy, we would say she has a strong *external* locus of control. We like to think of locus of control as a continuum. Consider where on the continuum you most often fall when something good happens.

Now think about where the members of your team may fall on this locus of control continuum. We contend that your employees will feel more energized and empowered to do their jobs when they have a higher *internal* locus of control. Over 30 years of research on locus of control has repeatedly shown a strong correlation between how much control an employee feels at work and that employee's degree of performance, effort, motivation, and satisfaction. In addition, researchers have found that a greater sense of control serves as a buffer against other situations that stress people out at work.

However, what gets in the way of employees having a sense of control over their work is often their manager. Twenty-plus years ago a manager's role was often described as consisting of three activities: planning, organizing, and controlling. For many a control freak that last descriptor was interpreted as permission to micromanage. Today we know that the more we let employees control their own work, the more productive they will be.

Control Freak Downsides	Autonomy Freak Upsides
• Employees stop taking initiative and only do what they are told.	• Employees find ways to improve how work is performed.
• Employees are afraid to take risks.	• Employees are willing to take calculated risks.
• Employees remain idle until they get the next set of instructions.	• Employees are able to continue their work even in your absence.

You may be familiar with the business mantra "do, delegate, defer, or drop." Everything on your to-do list can be sorted into one of these four categories. Unfortunately, the hardest one for many managers is delegate, even though we know that delegating is an effective way to manage our workload and develop others. You probably already are aware if you have control freak proclivities at work because they tend to show up at home too.

For many business leaders, giving up control or letting go can be difficult, as it was for our client Tim. By age 29, Tim had taken the helm of a company with $70 million in revenues. He got to that position because he showed leadership ability and produced great results. Tim liked being in control, but knew he needed to get out of the weeds and let go of some pet projects if he was truly going to lead the company.

If an Employee Seems Checked Out, Check Your Own Behavior First

Other business leaders have a hard time letting go because they are perfectionists, and we now know that perfectionism is the enemy of productivity (see Chapter 1).

"If you want something done right, you have to do it yourself," our client Mia, who runs a large design firm, told us.

However, insisting on doing things her way was beginning to cost her dearly. Deadlines were missed, and quality was slipping. She came to us for coaching because she was frustrated with her employees. "They just don't take initiative. And when they do, look what I get back," she said, sliding a PowerPoint presentation covered in red across the desk.

After interviewing her employees, we had to deliver the hard truth: "They've stopped taking initiative because they know whatever they produce will never be good enough because it's not exactly the way you would do things."

Mia wasn't buying it. "I like things done my way. Isn't that why employees are called subordinates?"

"Getting your employees to do things your way may satisfy the perfectionist in you, but over time, good employees will become disengaged or, worse yet, may leave and go to a competitor," we said.

"Actually, I have noticed that one of my employees, Jason, seems checked out. When I first hired him, I thought he had such potential. Now he responds to my requests with 'Whatever you want, boss.' He only does what he is asked and rarely takes initiative anymore. I'm at a loss," Mia said as she sank back in her chair.

We asked Mia to look inward and consider how she might be contributing to Jason's drop in performance. Mia had what we like to call an *aha moment*. Her control freak tendencies were creating the very behaviors she abhorred in others.

We left her with one other little piece of advice: "And by the way, get rid of that red pen. It reminds people of their evil English teacher."

The next time you find yourself in a similar situation, talk to your employee and find out what you can do differently, the way Mia did.

"I've noticed that you don't seem to enjoy your work as much as you used to," Mia observed in her next one-on-one with Jason. "Maybe I've been micromanaging. What can I do differently?"

"Why don't you try giving me the assignment with a specific due date and trust that I'll give it my best thinking and will ask you if I need help?" Jason replied.

Mia agreed to his request: "Okay, I'm going to delegate this piece of work to you. Here's what I'm looking for as an outcome. How you get it done is up to you. I trust you will ask me if you need any help."

Before Mia ended the meeting, she asked for some help herself. She knew a lifetime of micromanaging wasn't going to change in a day, a week, or even a month. She knew she needed a way to get real-time feedback so that she didn't slip back into old behaviors.

"If I start to angle my way in and try to take over, what's a code word or phrase you can say to remind me to back off?" she asked.

"How about 'freak off'?" Jason asked with a smile.

If you find it difficult to think of work you could let go of, simply ask your employees. You'll be surprised at how many tasks or projects you can delegate.

Although you may think you will be able to get more done by micromanaging, it will backfire. Employees work best when they have some sense of control over their work. Provide the training and coaching they need and then get out of their way so that they can shape the way they do their work.

KEY TAKEAWAYS

You have more influence on your employees' productivity than you may realize. From the moment you walk into work, the kind of mood you're in matters. Because your moods are more contagious than those of your employees, you need to be mindful of what you're transmitting. Infect your department, team, or office with positive emotions and keep your negative emotions at bay. Specifically, do the following:

- **Recognize the Achoo! effect.** Remember, your moods are contagious. You can't afford to stay in a bad mood for very long because it adversely affects not only your own productivity but that of your employees.

- **Tame your Oscar the Grouch if you need to.** We'd like to think we can model a positive mood all the time, but that's not always possible. When you find yourself in a foul mood, remember that a number of techniques have been proven to be effective to get you out of it: label your emotion, take a few deep breaths, get off your tush, and when all else fails, fake it till you make it.

- **Don't be a control freak.** If you suffer from control freak tendencies, your results and those of your team will suffer too. Instead, delegate and then get out of the way so that your employees can do their jobs.

● ● ● REFLECTION QUESTIONS ● ● ●

After reading this chapter, ask yourself these questions:

1. What am I already doing right to be a contagious, positive leader?

2. What triggers my negative moods, and how can I neutralize them?

3. Which of the four techniques for taming my Oscar the Grouch works best for me?

4. Whom do I trust to give me honest feedback about how I am perceived by others?

5. Under what circumstances do I tend to micromanage, and what can I do to combat this tendency?

6. What is one small change I can make that will help me better manage my emotions and create a more positive, productive workplace?

The Strengths-Based Leader:
Capitalize on What's Right

Now that you've mastered the behaviors of a productive, resilient, and contagious leader, there's one more attribute you must cultivate to be successful. Visionary? No. Innovative? Not quite. Charismatic? Not even close. We call it the *strengths-based leader*.

Imagine that you're an architect who designs bridges. How would you learn about the best bridges to build? Would you study all the bridges that have collapsed or all the bridges that have withstood the test of time? You probably would study both. However, too often we focus only on the bridges that have collapsed.

Similarly, leaders often study and try to fix only what's broken. In contrast, strengths-based leaders focus more of their attention on what's going right and then replicate those best practices in other areas. Strengths-based leaders don't ignore problems; rather, they recognize that solving problems and shoring up weaknesses are only part of the results equation.

Strengths-based leaders also focus more of their attention on what people do well (their strengths) rather than on what they don't do so well (their weaknesses).

Traditional Versus Strengths-Based Leader

Being a strengths-based leader may sound easy enough, but there are four obstacles to actually becoming one: we hate managing others, we love to solve problems, we treat employees as problems, and our brains are hardwired to the negative.

We hate managing others. Okay, maybe not hate, but some of us really don't like it. Why? Because many of us were promoted to management positions as a reward for excelling at our jobs. We were the best salesperson, the best technician, or the best analyst. Although managing others may not have played to our strengths or even desires, we accepted the management role because of the lure of more pay, more perks, and more prestige. Consequently, for some of us, leading others actually removes us from the work we most enjoy. It takes a courageous leader to admit to himself and his boss that he may be happier to return to the work he finds most satisfying.

We love to solve problems. "My role is to analyze problems and then find solutions," says one of our clients, a woman who manages a team of testers. "Isn't that what I'm paid to do?"

We treat employees as problems. Although solving problems may be the primary focus of many roles, the trouble comes when this fix-it mindset spills over into the way managers view employees. Some subscribe to the notion that employees must be fixed, motivated, or watched every minute in order to get them to perform.

Our brains are hardwired to the negative. Even if we love managing people and view our jobs as more than solving problems, becoming a strengths-based leader may still be a challenge. Some researchers argue that there is an evolutionary component to why we focus more on what's wrong than on what's right. For early humans to survive, they had to keep their eyes peeled for danger, not for a beautiful sunset. In their journal article "Bad Is Stronger Than Good," Baumeister and his colleagues refer to this phenomenon as *negativity bias*. People react much more strongly to losing a $20 bill from their wallets than to finding a $20 bill on the street. People ruminate on a negative comment from a friend for much longer than they bask in a compliment. And customers tell 13 people on average when they have a bad experience with a company but tell only 5 people when they receive stellar service.

MAGNIFYING THE NEGATIVE

What do you tend to focus on when you receive your:

- Performance review or 360-degree feedback results? Do you skip right over your strengths and go directly to your weaknesses or areas for development?

- Employee survey results? Do you skim over what's going right and fixate on the bottom 10 percent?

Curious to know how well a strengths-based approach fits with your own leadership style? Take the quick manager self-assessment in Appendix B or on our website ProfitFromThePositive.com: "Is a Strengths-Based Approach a Good Fit for Me?"

Perhaps you are leading from a place of strengths already and may have picked up *Profit from the Positive* to learn even more. Maybe viewing your leadership role from a strengths perspective is a significant paradigm shift for you. Regardless of how natural becoming a strengths-based leader is for you, in this chapter we show you how to add to your arsenal of problem-solving skills by mining your own company for what's going right. We also demonstrate how you can increase your team's performance by nearly 40 percent simply by the way you react to bad news. Lastly, we give you a three-minute, no-cost way to uncover your own strengths first so that you can lead the way in your company.

1. STOP ASKING THE WRONG QUESTIONS

Most of us are fairly adept at studying what's wrong. We are trained to analyze problems, identify root causes, brainstorm possible solutions, and then implement the best approach. Most consulting has traditionally relied on this problem-solving model. We improve results by removing one problem after another. This is crucial for companies to do and do well. Although this problem-solving method works, there is another way to improve results that we often neglect.

We don't apply the same rigor to studying and capitalizing on what's going right. Imagine that you have a department, location, or region that gets exceptional results compared with others. Imagine analyzing what specifically it does so that you can replicate those practices in other areas. We often take this approach when studying our competitors, but we fail to apply this "what's working" analysis to our own company. And even if we do, when we try to implement these best practices in other areas, we are often met with resistance, or what we call the "that won't work here" syndrome.

Research by New York University psychology professor Tory Higgins and his colleagues found that people tend to be in one of two mental states: either *excited* about moving toward a wanted and desirable outcome or *cautious* about avoiding an unwanted and undesirable result. This cautious mindset is highly effective for maintaining the status quo and avoiding risk. However, if you're like most companies, you have challenging goals to meet. You will probably need many of your people to be in an excited and moving-forward state. Higgins and his colleagues found that when people focus on what they most desire and remind themselves of their ideals and aspirations, they are more energized to make changes and take action. When you evaluate exceptional results, you are more likely to make changes than you are when you evaluate problems and areas of caution.

Be a Copycat

Ask questions that get at why one area, team, or person is out-performing another; share those success stories; and then replicate those practices in other areas.

BE A MINER: QUESTIONS TO SHINE A LIGHT ON WHAT'S RIGHT

Mine your company, team, or department for what's going right:

- Where is this change or process being implemented well, and what can we learn that we could apply to other areas?

- What is it about this employee that makes her successful in this role?

- Why does this team or location consistently exceed expectations?

That's what NUMMI (New United Motor Manufacturing Inc.), a joint venture between Toyota and GM, did to improve processes. NUMMI was actually two companies in one building. One company built the Toyota Tacoma truck, and the other built the Toyota Corolla and the Pontiac Vibe. For many years the truck company outperformed the car company. A former employee told us, "One day our VP of manufacturing decided he wanted the car-side managers to observe the truck-side managers and their team members to see why they were outperforming." The vice president said, "Why should we send the car-side employees to another Toyota car plant in Kentucky or Canada to find ways of improving processes when they can just go observe the truck side right here in our own plant?"

The larger your company, the greater the chance that there are boundaries or silos between divisions, departments, and teams. Why? As companies grow, we tend to organize people into separate departments to be most efficient. If you are willing to break down these artificial silos, you can uncover what's going right and apply what you learn to your business.

Success Stories

We were helping our client design a national sales meeting. Two weeks before the meeting, we solicited success stories from the field. We asked attendees to send us a quick email about a recent positive event or someone they wanted to recognize. There were 10 geographic territories. After a week's time we had heard from only four areas. These were salespeople, and so we knew that a little competition might spur them to action. We sent out a reminder and offered a prize for the best story. The stories started to pour in.

The conference committee then picked eight stories to read over the course of the two-day meeting. They called the lucky winners to tell them their stories had been selected. We had the remaining stories printed on posters, and on the eve of the conference we displayed the success stories in the hallway. We called it the Hall of Fame. When the salespeople walked in that first morning, they were struck by the stories. This wasn't going to be the same old, same old sales conference.

SOAR, Don't SWOT

You can also bring a more strengths-based approach to your business planning. The next time you bring your team together to develop your strategy or plan, break from the traditional SWOT analysis (*s*trengths, *w*eaknesses, *o*pportunities, and *t*hreats) and facilitate a SOAR analysis instead: *s*trengths, *o*pportunities, *a*spirations, and *r*esults.

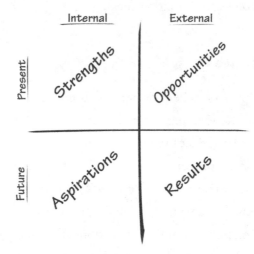

SOAR Analysis

We facilitated a SOAR analysis when our client convened her more than 75 managers from various service centers around the country for their annual fall planning meeting. "We broke into small groups to discuss the implications of what we learned from earlier strategy discussions," our client, Ally, recalled, "and we used the SOAR analysis as a way to structure our thinking."

What did they come up with? "When we did the debrief, a number of themes emerged from the SOAR," Ally explained. "Strengths included our talented people, our brand with brokers, and our financial discipline. Opportunities included self-service capacity, website enhancements, and customer analytics."

"What surprised you the most, Ally?" we asked.

"Probably the *aspirations*. We had never really talked about them before. What we took away from the session was a 'be the brand' aspiration, meaning we live it and make every customer interaction really personal."

"What about the discussion of *results*?" we asked.

"That was a really positive discussion," she replied. "It engaged my colleagues and focused us toward more growth without increasing expenses. We also realized from our SOAR analysis that while we have a strong brand with our brokers, we want to build a strong brand in our community."

Let's face it, in a SWOT analysis, weaknesses are typically the flip side of strengths and threats are usually the flip side of opportunities. Engage your team members in a more positive and empowering discussion about what they aspire to be and the kinds of results they seek.

You may be thinking that a SOAR analysis ignores the negative. Not true. Weaknesses and threats are discussed but then reframed during the discussion of *opportunities*. For example, in Ally's organization, the website hadn't been updated in years and the company wasn't leveraging its customer analytics as well as its competitors were. These were clearly weaknesses and possibly even threats, but in the SOAR discussion they were reframed as opportunities, which allowed people to become energized—as opposed to resigned—to address them.

Most Project Reviews Are Broken

When we first started working with the IT leadership team at a large insurer, we asked them to share with us the methods they use to improve performance. "We have weekly project review meetings," the head of the department offered.

We were curious. "Tell us how you run those meetings."

"We bring in project teams that have been identified as in the red, meaning they're *off track*, and we discuss ways to get them back on track."

"Okay, that sounds reasonable," we said. "But what about the teams that are *on track*? Do they come in too to share what's working?"

The lightbulb went off. "I think our project reviews are broken," said one manager. "They tend to be punitive, and we never ask about what's going right. In fact, we call them 'postmortems,' and I've heard employees call them 'the principal's office' meetings because that's what they feel like."

But let's not be naive. Things go wrong every day in business, not to mention in life. Milestones get missed. Systems break down. Customers get angry and threaten to leave. Do we ignore these problems? No. In the next tool, learn how to respond to bad news in a way that will boost, not deflate, your team's productivity.

2. FIND SOLUTIONS, NOT FAULTS

We are not advocating that you focus only on what's going right. We know that people can always learn from their mistakes. However, the way you respond to your employees when they come to you with problems really does matter (see Chapter 3). Flying off the handle will do nothing to get you out of the mess you're in.

In a research study Margaret conducted with our University of Pennsylvania classmate Dana Arakawa, we asked over 80 IT employees how their manager reacts when a problem crops up. The participants indicated their agreement with statements such as, "My project manager is able to put it in perspective for me," and "My project manager is able to help me come up with solutions." Their responses to these and other statements were then compared with the performance of the projects they worked on. Project performance was measured by how well these projects met budget, schedule, and quality standards. Margaret and Dana found that managers who scored in the top quartile for brainstorming solutions with their employees while keeping their cool saw a 39 percent increase in project performance compared with managers who scored in the bottom quartile.

Some managers, in an effort to avoid problems from being dumped on their desks, tell employees, "Don't come to me with a problem unless you can propose a solution." This is flawed logic. Sometimes employees need to talk through some potential solutions with you. If you expect your employees to always have the answer, you may learn about problems much too late to do anything about them, as this system analyst in our study explained:

"My project manager tends to overreact initially and then calms down once the situation is fully explained. Because of this, my team and I tend not to go to him about a problem unless we have some kind of idea of the solution already or unless the problem is very important."

If you're frustrated that you chronically hear about bad news too late to do anything about it, it may be because your employees are afraid to come to you. Instead, help your employees explore other perspectives (as you learned in Chapter 2) and find solutions.

Don't become another problem for your employees to handle the way our client Carlos was at one time.

Encourage Bad News

Carlos is frustrated, maybe even furious. He just learned that his project is delayed by four weeks. Even worse, the first he learns of the delay is not from his team but from his peer at his boss's weekly staff meeting. Carlos came to a coaching call and said, "If only my employees would come to me sooner, I could do something about the problem. When they do finally come to me, I'm at my wit's end."

We gave Carlos an assignment: "The next time this happens, and you know there will be a next time, focus on solutions." At his next coaching session we asked him to share what had happened.

DON'T PLAY THE BLAME GAME: QUESTIONS THAT PROMOTE SOLUTIONS AND OWNERSHIP

Encourage your employees to come to you with problems, and ask questions like these:

- Without placing blame, how do you think we got here?

- Let's brainstorm some solutions. What are some short-term possibilities? Long-term?

- If you ran the zoo, what would you do?

"I acknowledged that none of us likes to disappoint our customers, but together we can work this out," Carlos explained.

"I also made it clear that pointing fingers was going to get us nowhere. Instead we brainstormed some solutions and ended up running with one of them. I closed the meeting by asking the team to think about what we can do to prevent this from happening in the future."

Now that you are armed with some ways to approach problems differently, there's one more thing you must know to be a strengths-based leader: your own strengths.

3. KNOW YOUR STRENGTHS OR NO ONE ELSE WILL

Visitors to the ancient Greek town of Delphi will see the words *"Nosce te ipsum"* inscribed over the entrance to the Temple of Apollo. Know thyself. To become a strengths-based leader, you must know thyself. Specifically, you must truly know your own strengths.

Focusing on what you do well—your strengths—isn't another fad. We now have data from a wide range of industries that point to many positive business outcomes. From boosting sales, to improving customer service, to enhancing innovation, to increasing employee engagement, strengths have been shown to work. For example, Gallup conducted a study with Marriott Vacation Club salespeople. The salespeople completed a 40-minute strengths assessment followed by a one-on-one discussion of their strengths with their manager. The bottom line? This group of salespeople brought in 17 percent more sales compared with those who didn't complete the strengths assessment. If implemented across the board, this increase in sales would result in millions of dollars at each location. Even U.S. Army recruits are learning how to use their strengths. About one million soldiers have participated in the Comprehensive Soldier Fitness program that includes a self-assessment of their resilience strengths.

Survey Says

When we think of Gallup, most of us think of the polling company. But a big part of Gallup's business over the last 40 years has involved the study of human strengths. Gallup interviewed nearly 200,000 employees in 36 companies and found that one question was most predictive of low employee turnover, high employee engagement, and a high employee success rate. What was the question? "Do you like your boss?" No. "Are you satisfied with your pay?" No. The question was about using their strengths: "At work do you have the opportunity to do what you do best every day?"

Sadly, only 20 percent of employees globally believe that they have the chance to do what they do best every day. However, Gallup found that in business units in which employees had the opportunity to do what they do best every day, they experienced an increase in productivity, customer loyalty, and employee retention.

Steve Jobs on Jobs

As Steve Jobs, former Apple CEO, said in his commencement speech at Stanford, "For the past 33 years, I have looked in the mirror every morning and asked myself: 'If today were the last day of my life, would I want to do what I am about to do today?'"

Jobs asked himself this question long before he knew of his illness. "And whenever the answer has been 'No' for too many days in a row, I know I need to change something."

This doesn't mean that you change jobs every time things are not perfect. If you hate your job, maybe it would help to think of new and creative ways to use your strengths.

Not a Program du Jour

Becoming a strengths-based leader isn't about implementing some program du jour. It's a way of being—a way of leading. Leaders must first acknowledge and model their own strengths. Only then can a leader truly appreciate and leverage the strengths of others.

THREE MINUTES, NO COST: QUESTIONS TO UNCOVER YOUR STRENGTHS

A simple way to identify your strengths is to ask yourself these questions:

- What am I really good at?

- What kind of work really energizes me?

- When am I at my best?

Once you ask yourself these questions, go ask some of your colleagues, employees, friends, and family members. See what comes up again and again. These are your strengths. Martin Seligman clarifies, "Working hard to manage weaknesses, while sometimes necessary, will only help us prevent failure. It will not help us reach excellence."

A more thorough approach to uncovering your strengths is to take an actual *strengths assessment*. The good news is that you have some no-cost or low-cost options, two of which take approximately 30 minutes to complete online:

- Visit www.viasurvey.org and complete the VIA Inventory of Strengths Survey. As soon as you click on the "Submit" button, you will receive a free results report. If you prefer a more detailed report, you will be sent one for $40.

- Purchase the book *StrengthsFinder 2.0* (Rath) or *Strengths Based Leadership: Great Leaders, Teams, and Why People Follow* (Rath and Conchie). An access code in the back of the book will allow you to go online and complete the assessment at no additional cost. Again, as soon as you hit the "Submit" button, you will receive a comprehensive strengths report.

- Don't want to buy another book? Visit www.gallup strengthscenter.com/purchase instead and for under $10 you can take the online assessment and receive your Strengths Discovery Package.

So I Know My Strengths: Now What?

This is often a question we get when we first introduce our clients to strengths. They want to know how they can benefit from this newfound knowledge. We suggest that they begin by looking back.

"How have you used your strengths in the last day or week?" we asked our client Terry, who heads operations at a Fortune 500 company.

A WORD ABOUT SELF-ASSESSMENTS

We probably all have known people who take a self-assessment and then become zealots, believing that the assessment explains all human behavior. Don't turn strengths into just another fad. Regardless of which strengths self-assessment you use, be aware of the following questions:

- **If I take this assessment again, will I get the same results?** Often, the answer is no. Thus, when you draw conclusions that are based on your results, be aware that these conclusions are not written in stone.

- **Does this assessment seem to be measuring what it claims to measure?** The answer can be no, and so you should be cautious about overrelying on the results.

- **Will having the results of this assessment help me predict how I will perform in certain situations?** Be open to the fact that the results may be informative but are not foolproof, and do not assign the assessment more power than it deserves.

Terry told us, "I've noticed that in the last week, I have used my *curiosity* strengths in really getting to know my two new employees. I've also noticed that I'm really energized when I ask probing questions during our operational review meetings."

After he looked back, we asked Terry to look ahead. "Let's identify some situations, projects, or work challenges where you can use one of your strengths even more over the next week or two."

"I have a number of meetings coming up this week where I really need to understand the business requirements before my team and I can move forward. I'm going to turn the volume up on my curiosity strength."

Once you understand and model your strengths, you are ready to introduce this concept to your employees. In Chapter 6, you'll learn how. But before we go there, find out what you need to know about hiring the right team. Even if you don't have plans or a budget to hire employees any time soon, you will still find Chapter 5 useful.

KEY TAKEAWAYS

Strengths-based leaders don't ignore problems, but they do capitalize on what's right. Add to your tool kit these simple yet powerful ways to boost performance:

- **Stop asking the wrong questions**. Fixing what's broken is one way to improve performance, but don't forget to apply the same rigor to understanding what's behind exceptional performance. Ask questions that shed light on what's going right and then use this knowledge to implement best practices.

- **Find solutions, not faults.** Problems can be unpredictable, but the way you respond to them doesn't have to be. Encourage your employees to come to you when problems arise. Remain calm and help your employees find solutions.

- **Know your strengths or no one else will.** Before you can introduce the concept of strengths to your company or team, it's important that you understand your own strengths first. Only then can you truly appreciate and leverage the strengths of others.

Remember, becoming a strengths-based leader may be natural for you or it may require more effort. Put these three tools into action to achieve better results.

● ● ● REFLECTION QUESTIONS ● ● ●

After reading this chapter, ask yourself these questions:

1. What am I already doing right to be a strengths-based leader?

2. How can I learn more about my strengths?

3. Where are we achieving our best results, and what can we learn from this?

4. How do I react when presented with problems or bad news? What do I need to change?

5. How can I bring a more strengths-based approach to one or more of our business practices, such as project reviews?

6. What is one small change I can make that will help me become more of a strengths-based leader?

PART II

It's
About
the
Team

This section focuses on what you can do to boost your team's performance and transform your business. As a leader, you juggle many responsibilities. There's no way you can do it alone. You must rely on your team to come up with innovative ideas, serve customers, collaborate with other departments, and deliver products or services on time and on budget. We show you how to apply positive psychology findings to four common business practices to bring out the best in your team.

After reading this section, you will be able to:

- **Make better hiring decisions** (Chapter 5). For example, did you know that technical skills, experience, and education account for only half of the success equation?

- **Improve performance** (Chapter 6). For example, did you know that you can boost productivity by over 40 percent simply by giving frequent recognition and encouragement?

- **Achieve greater results** (Chapter 7). For example, did you know that *pre*viewing performance rather than *re*viewing performance can produce better outcomes?

- **Get the most out of your meetings** (Chapter 8).
  For example, did you know the *magic ratio* for high-performing teams?

In each chapter, we share with you the latest research followed by practical tools you can implement today. Go ahead; turn the page.

HIRING:
The Fitness Test

"**He had all the right skills** and experience, but he just didn't work out."

Tired of spending big bucks on recruiting firms? Tired of starting the recruiting process all over again when your superstars fail to shine? Need to hire a team fast for the new business you are launching? Hiring mistakes are costly. Studies by a human resources consulting company found that every hire costs a company up to five times the person's salary when you add in benefits, training, and other soft costs. Zappos.com CEO Tony Hsieh says, "If you add up all the bad decisions of the bad hires made . . . in the course of Zappos's history, it's probably cost us over $100 million."

We coach business leaders from both sides of the desk: those who are hiring and those who are interviewing for their own next career opportunity. We've found four common mistakes hiring managers make: we don't prepare well for the interview and instead wing it, we talk too much, we mistakenly believe that technical skills trump interpersonal skills, and we look for talent only when we need it.

We wing it. We schedule time on our calendars to interview candidates, but we invest little or no time preparing. Instead, we walk into the interview having only glanced at the candidate's resume and then ask the same old generic prompts or questions, such as, "Walk me through your resume," and, "What is your biggest weakness?" In Senia's research with her colleagues at Stanford, she found that people are drawn to the familiar even though staying with the familiar may harm progress toward the original goal. Similarly, we rely on the same familiar interview questions even when they may hinder learning more about a candidate to determine if there is a good fit.

We talk too much. We spend too much time talking about ourselves, the position, and the company and not enough time listening to really get to know the candidate. Sometimes we don't ask follow-up questions to dig deeper or allow enough time for the candidate to ask us questions. We can learn a great deal about candidates not only from how they answer our questions but from the questions they ask us. While searching for his next big career move, one corporate leader told us, "I was surprised that at my last interview, they didn't ask me why I wanted to leave my current employer. If they had, they would have learned about the kind of leader I am and what I value. Instead, the hiring manager spoke a lot about the company, which was great to hear, but I don't think they got a strong sense of whether I would be a good fit or not."

We believe technical skills trump interpersonal skills. Many hiring managers think that if they seek out the technical skills, experience, and educational level outlined in the job description, they'll be able to make a great hire. Not so fast. One of the main qualities most employers want is the candidate's ability to work well with others. You're not going to be able to assess this interpersonal skill very well from a resume. The candidate may look like a star on paper, but it's the personal interview that will help you decide if that star is well aligned in your company's solar system.

We don't scout talent. Instead, we hire only when we need to. You may be thinking that hiring is not so relevant when the economy is down and when budgets are tight. You may be wondering why we're devoting a chapter to hiring practices rather than layoff practices. The logic is simple. A down economy is an excellent time to do exploratory interviews and bring in strong candidates if you can. When unemployment is high, you as the hiring manager can do the following:

- **Pick from an Olympic-sized candidate pool.** Many people will be applying for your open positions. You can screen and choose the best candidate for the job.

- **Capitalize on low employee engagement at other companies.** High performers often become dissatisfied with company cutbacks. They see their careers stalling. You may be able to lure strong candidates away from their current employers by offering them opportunities to grow and develop.

- **Attract internal transfers**. Employees at your company often look for opportunities in other business units or departments rather than at your competitors. You may be able to attract them to your department, especially if you are known for being a great leader or developer of people.

In this chapter, we show you how to avoid these common pitfalls and make better hiring decisions. We call it the *fitness test*. Fit can be measured by how well a potential candidate aligns with the job itself and with your company or department. Learn how to hire for what's *not* on the resume and ask interview questions that are most predictive of success. We also share with you some secrets successful companies use to avoid costly hiring mistakes.

1. HIRE FOR WHAT'S NOT ON THE RESUME

Martin Seligman struck up a conversation with the man sitting next to him on the plane. The man happened to be the CEO of MetLife and happened to have a problem: he was not able to hire and retain enough competent salespeople. Life insurance sales is typically one of the most challenging jobs because of the constant rejection salespeople face. Rarely does a prospective customer respond to a sales call with, "Yes, I'm just dying to buy some life insurance." The MetLife CEO needed to reduce turnover and keep his salespeople resilient in the face of rejections.

Seligman proposed a solution to the CEO: MetLife should hire people from two distinct groups and see which group produces the most sales and has the highest retention rate. MetLife hired 1,000 new recruits, all of whom had passed its insurance career profile test. At the same time it hired an additional 129 salespeople who had barely passed the insurance career profile but had passed an optimism test with flying colors. All 1,129 new recruits went out into the field, but no recruit or his manager was told about the two groups and the distinction between them. What happened? Two years later, the 129 recruits who had scored high on the optimism test outperformed the other group by a 27 percent increase in sales.

We know that burnout and turnover are rampant in many jobs like sales, and a trait such as resilience can be a predictor of success. After reading Chapter 2, you know it's a predictor of your success too. But how can you hire for skills, such as resilience, that don't necessarily appear on the resume? Make sure your next new hire can pass your fitness test.

Senia wasn't always a believer in fit. She was introduced to the notion of fit by her Stanford professor and business consultant Jeffrey Pfeffer in an MBA course on human resource management. Pfeffer clearly laid out the business case for hiring not only for technical skills but also for attitude and soft skills that fit with the company's culture. "Having worked at Morgan Stanley, I walked out of the program still convinced that hiring for skills, such as project management, financial analysis, or programming, took precedence over an intangible like fit. It was only later, in coleading a high-tech start-up in the Boston area that I became convinced."

In a start-up, agile thinking and the ability to quickly change directions are essential. Programmers who are successful in this kind of environment are able to rapidly switch gears and adapt to change.

Senia went on to explain, "My company had a handful of programmers. When clients' needs changed or project specs differed from the original designs, I clearly saw that the programmers who performed the best were those who had a start-up mindset. They fit with not only the position requirements but with our company. That's when I became a convert to fit and began hiring for what was not on the resume."

The Soft Stuff Is the Hard Stuff

In a review of job descriptions at over 100 Fortune 500 companies, emotional intelligence author and psychologist Daniel Goleman found that only one-third of the skills or competencies required were technical in nature, whereas two-thirds were interpersonal in nature. Unfortunately, when we interview candidates, we tend to overly focus on the one-third—the technical skills. Don't. Pay attention to the other, less tangible qualities such as the candidate's ability to collaborate, manage stress, and take initiative.

Taking initiative, for example, has been shown to correlate with productivity according to researcher Michael Frese from the University of Giessen in Germany. If you're recruiting for a job that requires initiative, interview for that quality. Simply ask the candidate to tell you about the last time she took something upon herself and made it happen.

Some people refer to qualities such as initiative, collaboration, and empathy as soft skills. But more often than not, the soft stuff is the hard stuff, meaning that the soft skills are more difficult to train. Hire for these soft skills now. If you don't, you'll be dipping into your training budget later or dealing with chronic interpersonal issues that often don't end well.

"I'll hire someone with a positive, can-do attitude and no phone skills before I'll hire someone with a lot of customer service experience who has a poor attitude," Chris Beschler, deputy chief administrative officer of operations for the city of Richmond, Virginia, told us. "Give me someone with a positive attitude, and I can teach them how to use our phone system."

Some very successful companies do ask questions to get at what's not on the resume. For example, Microsoft CEO Steve Ballmer said, "I try to figure out sort of a combination of IQ and passion. I just ask somebody to tell me what they've done that they are really proud of. . . . "This question can uncover the candidate's values, such as autonomy, teamwork, and perseverance. If these qualities are needed to be successful in the job you are seeking to fill, interview for them until you get a match.

A Word of Caution on Preemployment Assessments

We are often asked if we recommend using any preemployment assessments to help screen candidates. The answer is: it depends. It depends on what you're trying to measure to determine fit. Keep in mind that many self assessments measure preferences rather than abilities. Always check with your HR and legal staff before administering any preemployment assessments.

2. PREDICT THE FUTURE BY DIGGING INTO THE PAST

Professor Amy Wrzesniewski at the Yale School of Management has studied various professions and has found that people view their work in three very different ways: as a *job*, a *career*, or a *calling*. Those who view their work as a job perform their work to pay the bills. Those who view their work as a career perform their work to get promoted and keep moving forward in their chosen profession. Those who view their work as a calling believe they are contributing to a larger, more meaningful purpose.

We often think that to perceive one's work as a calling one must be in a healing or ministering profession. Not true. What's interesting is that these three perspectives have nothing to do with the level of complexity or education associated with the work. For example, a hospital janitor in the study said he was helping the patients heal (a calling). Wrzesniewski found that people who see their work as a calling gain more meaning that leads them to want to perform their very best. You can hire people who view their work as a job, and they'll most likely get the job done. But you may need to attract more people who perceive their work as a career or a calling to really differentiate your company from your competitors.

Look at who performs the job really well today or treats his or her work as a career or calling. Also look at who may have performed this job well in the past (remember, you can learn from what's going right, as we pointed out in Chapter 4). Write down the attributes you noticed. If it's a new position, identify the attributes you think are necessary to be successful in the job and then validate them with others. Next, develop questions or prompts to uncover these attributes during candidate interviews. But not just any questions.

Question Your Questions

Our client Denise manages a team of 18 auditors in remote offices around the country. She was frustrated that turnover was at an all-time high. Sound judgment and the ability to make decisions independently are key competencies of a good auditor, Denise told us. One of the questions we learned that she always asked candidates was: "*What would you* do if an urgent situation came up in which you had to make a decision that typically required my approval and I wasn't available?"

We helped Denise reword her question from *a future* orientation to a *past* orientation. If two different job candidates give great answers to "what would they do" types of questions, what does that tell you about them? Not very much other than that they are good conversationalists. But if two different job candidates describe how they actually handled an urgent situation when their boss wasn't around, you can discern which candidate best fits with your requirements.

Remember, *the best predictor of future performance is past performance*. Although "what-would-you-do" questions may reveal a candidate's creativity, they are also the easiest to fake. Use them sparingly. Instead use "what-have-you-done" questions.

Attributes You Need	Questions or Prompts to Uncover Them
• Initiative	• Describe for me a time in your career when you worked without any on-site management. What did you like about it? What didn't you like about it? How did you keep yourself motivated and meet deadlines? How did you keep your boss informed?
• Critical thinking	• Tell me about a problem you recently solved at work. What specifically did you do? What was the outcome?
• Collaboration	• Describe for me a time when you had to work with a difficult team member to achieve results. How did you handle that?

Now that you know how to frame interview questions to get at what's not on the resume and better predict how successful a candidate will be, there's one more technique you must know to make a great hiring decision.

3. DON'T OVERLOOK YOUR CULTURE'S QUIRKS

Google has a term for employees who fit the company's culture: *Googly*. Googly is a shorthand description for someone who is smart, creative, a good problem solver, and fun to be around. What's your company's version of Googly?

If you are planning a trip to Las Vegas, visit www.zapposin sights.com before you go to arrange a company tour. The Zappos van will pick you up and take you on a tour of its company headquarters. Zappos, the online retailer, was started in 1999. Ten years later, in the middle of a recession, it was bought by Amazon for about $1.2 billion. CEO Tony Hsieh and his team built Zappos by hiring people who fit not only with the job but with the company's core values.

Hsieh explains: "Today, when we interview, we have questions for each one of the core values. One of our values is, 'Create fun and a little weirdness.' So the question is: On a scale of 1 to 10, how weird are you? If you're a 1, you're probably a bit too strait-laced for us. If you're a 10, you might be too psychotic for us. It's not so much the number, it's more how candidates react. Because our whole belief is that everyone is a little weird, so it's really more just a fun way of saying that we recognize and celebrate each person's individuality and we want their true personality to shine in the workplace."

How well do Zappos's hiring practices work? Christa Foley, senior manager of HR at Zappos University, told us, "We have an engaged and empowered workforce that wants to be here. . . . It also leads to strong employee loyalty and low turnover."

Passion in the Workplace

If you hire people who fit well with your company's culture, they are more likely to be passionate about their work. Think of an employee who demonstrates zest or energy for your company. He is excited about the company's values, goals, and direction. A recent finding by our colleagues in positive psychology shows that zest— also called drive, energy, or passion—is the biggest contributor to enjoying one's work. Additionally, people who have zest have been found to be more psychologically healthy, and psychological health has been linked to improved job performance and reduced turnover, not to mention lower healthcare costs.

Here's an example of what you get when you hire people who fit with your culture's quirks:

"I found out today that it is a lot easier being a salesman for 3M than for a little company no one has ever heard of. . . . And I discovered I came across warmer and friendlier."

A group of researchers describe this comment as "strong identification" with the company. They argue that this 3M salesperson, along with others like him, believes that the traits of 3M—such as being innovative and successful—are traits that get transferred from the company to him. Passion for the company translates into passion and energy to perform one's job really well.

One of our clients, Josh, who runs a business-to-business software collaboration tool company, told us he looks for people who really know how to collaborate both in meetings and in day-to-day project work. "Our department is actually pretty casual, and we have many impromptu, fast brainstorming meetings," he explained. "I need to attract people who will thrive in this kind of environment."

Josh now uses this interview question to uncover a candidate's fit with his company: "Tell me about the office environment you work in today. How does work get done, and what do you like or not like about it?"

Go for More

Another way to find out if a candidate is truly a good fit not only for the job but also for your company is to go beyond the one-hour interview. Rackspace, a 2,000-employee web hosting company known for its impeccable customer service, says, "We'd rather miss a good one than hire a bad one." The company is divided into teams of 18 to 20 people, and many of the team members have become close friends outside of work. CEO Lanham Napier says that when teams interview candidates, they seek to get past the fake pleasantries. "They're here for nine or ten hours. . . . We're very cordial about it. We're not aggressive, but we haven't met a human being yet who has the stamina to BS us all day."

Now that you know how to recruit or attract strong people to your team, in Chapter 6 you will find out how to keep them highly engaged, productive, and fulfilled.

KEY TAKEAWAYS

Hiring people who fit well with both the requirements of the job and your company's culture is critical to your success. Be sure to hire only people who can pass your fitness test by doing the following:

- **Hire for what's not on the resume.** First do your homework. Begin by identifying the attributes necessary to be successful in the job you are looking to fill. Next, develop questions to uncover how well the candidate fits with these attributes. Pay attention not only to technical skills but to the more difficult-to-train interpersonal skills.

- **Predict the future by digging into the past.** The best predictor of future performance is past performance. Be sure you are asking "what-have-you-done" questions when you interview candidates.

- **Don't overlook your culture's quirks.** Do what Google does with Googly and what Zappos does with weirdness: do not shy away from asking questions that get at what makes your company or department unique.

Hiring for fit does not imply that there is one best candidate for whom you need to search high and low. It means that within your time and budget constraints, you search for and hire the best-fitting candidate. If you have candidates take your fitness test, it will save you time and dollars in the long run. You'll end up with a team of people who have not only the right skills but also the desire to perform their very best and enjoy working together. Don't underestimate this.

● ● ● REFLECTION QUESTIONS ● ● ●

After reading this chapter, think of a position you'll be hiring for within the next quarter and ask yourself these questions:

1. Is there someone currently in this job who is highly successful? What exactly makes him or her successful? (If you don't know specifically, ask him or her.)

2. What are the three most important attributes or interpersonal skills needed to be successful in this job that go beyond technical skills, education, and experience? What three questions can I ask to see if a candidate possesses these skills?

3. What are three company or department values that are a must-have for a candidate to fit in? What three questions would I ask to see if a candidate possesses them?

4. How can I involve my team in the interview and selection process?

5. What is one small change I can make in the way I interview candidates that will help me make better hiring decisions?

Engaging Employees:
Bring Out the Best Versus Get the Most

Clients often ask us, "How can I get the most out of my people?" We suggest that they ask themselves a somewhat different question that doesn't conjure up images of sucking every last ounce of energy out of employees. We propose that they consider the following: "How can I get people to perform at their very best?"

The answer is simple: by identifying, cultivating, and using their strengths every day. Improving productivity by using a strengths approach results in an energy-producing work environment where employees *want* to do their very best and will go that extra mile to accomplish their work and more.

Sounds simple enough, but in reality, focusing on strengths is very difficult for some people, as we learned in Chapter 4. Remember the negativity bias? Many of us view the world through a deficit lens and are constantly asking questions such as, What's missing? What isn't right? What needs fixing? What are our gaps? We are good at finding fault.

One of our clients acquired another company. As part of the integration process, we brought together a small group of executives from the two companies to take an inventory of their management practices. "What tools or processes do you have available for your managers to help them improve their employees' performance?" asked the president of the acquiring company.

"We have a progressive discipline process," replied the head of human resources at the acquired company. Margaret nearly fell off her chair.

Most businesses have a well-thought-out and well-documented progressive discipline process. The process goes something like this: when an employee doesn't meet expectations, he receives a verbal warning for the first offense, followed by a written warning if he doesn't straighten out, and he's often "let go" if he doesn't improve. Improving an employee's performance by using progressive discipline is like improving one's golf game by hiring a coach who warns "Don't miss" before every swing. Instead of a well-thought-out *progressive discipline* process, imagine if your company had a well-thought-out *progressive feedback* process. What might that do to improve employee performance?

Forget About
Employee Satisfaction

Twenty years ago, most businesses focused on *employee satisfaction*. Surveys were designed to measure how content employees were with their manager, the food in the cafeteria, and even the chairs they sat in. Businesses thought that if employees were satisfied with their work environment, they would perform well. But the satisfaction measure left out an important factor: the link between enjoying one's job and the company's profitability.

Fast forward to the new millennium. Today, successful companies such as Best Buy and Ann Taylor, among others, are focusing instead on *employee engagement*: how involved, enthusiastic, and attached an employee is to her work, her colleagues, and her company, which in turn furthers the company's interests. Gallup, which has been researching human behavior since the middle of the twentieth century, has found in its studies of over 17 million employees worldwide that the higher an employee's engagement is, the more productive, customer-focused, and safety-conscious he is and the less likely he is to leave the company for a competitor.

What Highly Engaged Looks Like

"You can see those who are engaged and those who do just enough to not get fired," says one of our clients, Stephanie, a VP of information technology. "I have some highly engaged employees—they display enthusiasm, they're inquisitive, and they like learning new things."

What creates an engaged workforce? Although a number of factors determine an employee's level of engagement, Gallup has found that employees who have the opportunity to focus on their strengths every day are six times more likely to be engaged in their jobs. As an added bonus, these employees are three times as likely to report having an excellent quality of life. Think about it: we spend a good deal of our waking hours at work, and so work can have a profound impact—positive or negative—on the quality of our lives. Unfortunately, according to the latest Gallup global statistics, only 30 percent of employees worldwide are engaged in their jobs. One sure way to boost engagement is to help employees discover and apply their strengths.

Over the last decade much has been written about identifying and leveraging one's individual strengths. However, little has been written about how business leaders can successfully implement a strengths-based approach with their teams or at their companies. In this chapter, we show you how to turn strengths into a team sport. We also show you how to turn around poor performance by using a simple visual framework that will result in more engaged and energized employees. Lastly, we report on original research that shows how progressive feedback, or what we call FRE (Frequent Recognition and Encouragement), can increase productivity by over 40 percent without costing a dime.

1. DON'T JUST READ THE BOOK

Besides boosting sales, focusing on strengths has been found to improve customer service. Studies of more than 300,000 employees at 51 companies showed that work teams that scored above the median on the number of members who apply their top strengths every day had 44 percent higher customer loyalty and employee retention compared with those that did not.

In addition to increasing customer loyalty and employee retention, focusing on strengths has been found to improve productivity. We wanted to find out for ourselves. In the study we told you about in Chapter 4, Margaret and Dana Arakawa asked employees to rate their level of agreement with a series of statements such as, "My project manager matches my talents to the tasks that need to be accomplished," and, "My project manager encourages high performance by building on my strengths." Their answers to these and other questions were then compared with the success of the projects on which those employees worked.

Specifically, projects that were led by managers who scored in the top quartile for focusing on their employees' strengths achieved better results. How much better? Fifty percent better than projects led by managers who didn't focus on employee strengths.

After reading Chapter 4, you know how to identify your own strengths. Now it's time to introduce strengths to your employees. However, asking your employees to read a book or take an assessment to identify their strengths is only the first step. The really powerful next step is to talk to your employees about their strengths and how they can use them even more. Most of us can recall a manager who said, "Here, read this book," but then never took the time to discuss its contents. We were left wondering what specifically we were supposed to do with this newfound knowledge, and the manager was left wondering why people weren't implementing the book's advice. Don't fall into this trap.

Introducing strengths to your employees is an exercise in *self-discovery*. Your job is to guide the discussion. There are no right or wrong answers. What you're trying to do is deepen your employees' understanding of their strengths and then help them think of ways to use those strengths even more.

Job Crafting

In Chapter 5, we showed you how to assess both company fit and job fit during candidate interviews. However, once a person is hired, assessing fit becomes an ongoing process to ensure that employees are engaged and productive. One way to do that is to be sure that their strengths are aligned with the work they are being asked to perform. Positive psychologists call this *job crafting*. Job crafting refers to just about any change, large or small, that creates a better fit between the requirements of the job and the strengths of the employee performing it. Our University of Pennsylvania classmate Gordon Parry, president of the Aristotle Group, ran a job crafting study at a large company. Participants reported positive results including, "[This] helped me recognize my contributions" and, "I have recognized opportunities that I did not know existed."

One of our clients, Emann, decided to introduce strengths and job crafting to one of her remote employees, Randy. Randy worked in one of the regional offices that Emann rarely had the chance to visit anymore as a result of cutbacks.

Emann gave him some context, "Researchers have found that the more we apply what we're naturally good at—our strengths— the happier, more fulfilled, and more productive we are. I'd like you to complete this online assessment that will take approximately 30 minutes. In our next one-on-one, we'll set aside some time to discuss your results. I'll share my results, too."

At Randy's next one-on-one, Emann began by explaining the purpose: "After our call today, you'll have a better understanding of your strengths, how they fit together, and how you can apply them even more.

"Although all of these strengths may be important to you, I'd like you to pick one and tell me how you applied that strength yesterday at work. How about last week? What about at home or in your community?"

BE A JOB FITNESS COACH: QUESTIONS TO BRING OUT YOUR EMPLOYEES' BEST

In coaching hundreds of business leaders, we have found the following questions helpful in assessing how well employees' strengths fit with their current jobs. See which questions you can use to guide discussions with your employees:

- Tell me the kind of work that really energizes you—work you can't wait to dive into.

- Tell me the kind of work that drains you.

- How could you use your strengths in a new way at work?

- Name one task or activity that you don't like to do. How could you use one or more of your strengths to increase your enjoyment of this task? Is there someone else on the team who might enjoy this task more? If not, should we consider rotating this task so that no one person gets stuck with it?

- What's the smallest change you could make that could have the biggest positive impact on your work?

After Randy talked about his first strength, Emann repeated the process for his other four strengths and then discussed how all five work together. She wrapped up their conversation by gaining Randy's commitment to apply his strengths to a specific work challenge: "Let's think of an assignment to which you could apply one of your strengths. It could be one of your challenging projects, customers, business partners, or coworkers. What would you like to focus on?"

"I've been so wrapped up in creating these new workflows that I haven't reached out to my peers in the other regional offices," Randy admitted. "I could really ramp up my *communication* strength and schedule a call to share progress with them."

"That sounds like a great way to use your strength, Randy," Emann replied. "In our next one-on-one, let me know how it's going."

You can certainly introduce your employees to their strengths one person at a time the way Emann did. However, if you lead a team of people, you may prefer to introduce strengths to everyone at the same time. Let's see how and what you will gain.

2. TURN STRENGTHS INTO A TEAM SPORT

The added benefit of using a team approach to introduce your employees to strengths is that they will understand and value not only their *own* strengths but also those of their *teammates*. You might be thinking, So what? If you're like many business leaders we know, you probably spend more time than you would like playing referee for employees who don't get along. When team strengths are known, differences are understood and valued rather than becoming a source of conflict.

Who has time to pull his team off the floor to talk about strengths when there are deadlines to meet and customers to serve? Let's see how one of our clients, Mark, pulled his team together for a strengths discussion in the middle of a major integration project.

Mark knew that his team could be even more productive if only its members would collaborate more. He decided to take an hour or so to introduce his team to strengths. He talked about next year's deliverables and how the team could better leverage one another's strengths to achieve them. He began by introducing the concept of strengths to his team:

"I know we all have a lot of work on our plates, and taking time off to plan and get to know each other's strengths may seem like a luxury. However, I strongly believe that if we invest a bit of time up front in our own development, we'll reap the benefits down the road. I'd like you to complete this online assessment, which will take only about 30 minutes. At our next team meeting, we'll set aside some time to discuss our results."

Two weeks later Mark facilitated a meeting with his employees to help them understand how their strengths worked together: "Let's go around the room, and we'll each share one or two of our top strengths and how well we think they reflect who we are. I'll capture them on a flipchart as we go. Then we can talk about how we've used our strengths most recently."

Mark got the ball rolling by revealing his top two strengths. After all the members of the team had shared one or two strengths, Mark gained their commitment to apply their strengths to a specific business challenge.

Mark concluded by saying, "Now that we know each other's strengths, let's take a look at next year's deliverables and see how we can better position ourselves for success."

Celebrating Differences

"From earlier research we know great leaders never need to be well rounded, but great teams probably do," says Tom Rath, author of *StrengthsFinder 2.0* and coauthor of *Strengths Based Leadership*.

Facilitating a strengths discussion with your team is an effective way for everyone to see how well-rounded the team is and to appreciate those differences.

"Another interesting thing I learned when going through the strengths assessment with my project team is that most, if not all, of my IT counterparts had *ideation* [having creative or original ideas] in their top three strengths," says an IT project leader that we worked with. "I have *responsibility*, *discipline*, and all of those project-leader-type strengths. The comical thing that happened when we reviewed each other's strengths was that my team had greater insight into why I try to nail them down on delivery, and I had an epiphany as to why they were so hard to nail down. They are lofty thinkers who like to bounce a bunch of ideas around. We were able to laugh about it in hindsight but also have a better appreciation of what makes each of us tick for future reference."

Consider combining a strengths discussion with other work your team needs to accomplish, such as business planning. Or perhaps you're about to launch a new project team. Identifying people's strengths early on can accelerate the start-up process and help you assign roles and responsibilities. You can also initiate a strengths discussion with multiple cross-functional teams that need to work together more closely to achieve a common goal. A tool for conducting a strengths discussion with your team can be found in Appendix C and on our website ProfitFromThePositive.com.

Once you know your employees' strengths, you will be better equipped to align roles and responsibilities that truly energize them. Armed with this kind of information, you will be able to create an engaged workforce, which will in turn positively affect your bottom line.

But what if you have some people who just aren't performing? What do you do then? Read the next tool to find out.

3. DON'T FIRE POOR PERFORMERS; FIRE 'EM UP

If you're an entrepreneur, you keep a constant eye on the cash flow of your business. If you're part of a large organization, you keep a constant eye on your budget. Either way, you're paying attention to the bottom line. But what you may not know is that you can positively affect your bottom line by getting your employees into a state that psychologists call *flow*.

The psychologist Mihaly Csikszentmihalyi (pronounced *cheeks-sent-me-high*) was a rock climber for decades. He noticed that when he was out climbing, sometimes he was engaged to the point of being "in the zone." Csikszentmihalyi called that feeling *flow*. A telltale sign of this state is when you are so immersed in your work that you lose all track of time.

If you're like many leaders we work with, you probably have some highly engaged people. They love their work and regularly get themselves into a state of flow.

Go with the Flow

You likely also have some people who underperform. You know these employees are capable of much more, but they're not producing as much or as well as they could. You may also have some employees who were at one time high performers but don't seem as engaged as they used to be. Sure, there could be circumstances outside of work that are negatively affecting their performance. But too often we overlook the most common cause: *poor fit* between the skill level of the employee and the level of the challenge.

Although it may be quicker to write up or fire a poor performer, it's much more expensive. If you hired the employee, you have already invested time and money in someone you thought would work out. If you inherited the employee, you have a responsibility as his new manager to give him a chance to turn around his performance. Rather than trying to improve performance by using a progressive discipline approach, have a flow discussion instead, using the model below.

Flow Model

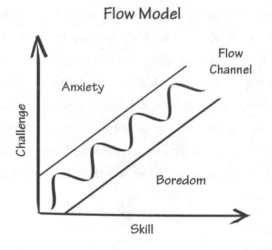

How does it work? When you give a task or job that is challenging to an employee whose skill level is low, she can become anxious and worry about making a mistake or completely failing. She will require more of your time and attention to become competent. Similarly, when you assign a task that is not very challenging to an employee whose skill level is high, you know it will get done right and probably get done faster than it would if you had given it to someone with less experience. But what you may not know is the negative effect this assignment has on the employee. You may get away with giving him these no-brainer assignments for a little while, but over time he will become bored and restless and may even begin looking for a job in which he can satisfy his need for challenging work.

We coach dozens of clients a year on how to use this flow model to turn around poor performance. One of our clients, Jill, had been getting complaints from her four sales reps that one of the inside sales guys, Steve, was not as efficient as he once had been. "He used to process my new business in 48 hours," one of the sales reps told her. "It's now taking Steve more than a week, and my new customers are not happy."

Rather than having a progressive discipline discussion, Jill decided to have a flow discussion instead. She started by acknowledging what she had noticed or heard: "Steve, the sales reps you support are not happy with your turnaround time. You used to be able to input new business into the system within 48 hours. Now it's taking more than five business days. What's getting in the way?"

Steve wasn't sure. "I'm just not as into it as I used to be."

That was when Jill decided to use the flow model to guide the discussion: "Let's see if we can figure this out together. I came across this chart recently, and I think it applies to many of us at different times in our careers. Take a look." Jill sketched out the flowchart for Steve. "We have the level of difficulty or challenge on the y axis and your skill level on the x axis. When it comes to processing new business, where do you think you are?"

Keep in mind that when you use this tool with your employees, there are no right or wrong answers. Once an employee acknowledges where he or she is on the flowchart, be sure to steer the conversation into concrete actions he can take to promote more of a flow state.

Jill went on to explain, "Not all of the work you do will produce a state of flow. Sometimes there are tasks we have to do that we may not like, but hopefully that's not a huge percentage of our time here at work. What could we do to help you get in the flow channel more often?"

Like Riding a Bike

You have numerous opportunities every day to help people find their flow state by designing work that fits their flow channel—just the right level of challenge to suit their skill level and strengths. Here's how one senior developer in the IT department of a Fortune 200 company described crafting his job with his manager:

"My manager and I can plot out where I can have the most impact, and I can expect to really enjoy the tasks that are in line with my strengths. We can also see where I just need to 'get through' some tasks that don't play to my strengths. Since we know this, I can anticipate where I need to apply more personal focus, energy, and positive spin to get the task out of the way versus letting the task sap my energy. I think of it like a bike ride. The downhills, strengths, are fun, and the uphills, not my strengths, can be conquered via effort, focus, and patience."

Sometimes when you've done all you can to encourage or fire up an employee, it still doesn't work. What do you do then? You can suggest that he rotate or post for jobs in other departments that better fit his strengths and will offer new challenges. If no opportunities exist within your company, it may be time to encourage the employee to find another job. Although this may be difficult in the short run, trust us, you'll both be happier in the long run. If your only alternative is to terminate the employee, be sure you have documented your efforts to prevent any legal hassles later on.

There's one more way to boost performance without dipping into your budget. We call it FRE: Frequent Recognition and Encouragement.

4. GIVE FRE: FREQUENT RECOGNITION AND ENCOURAGEMENT

Imagine that you could improve productivity by over 40 percent. It could potentially affect your speed to market, reduce your costs, increase your sales, or improve your ability to serve customers. Now imagine that you could achieve these productivity gains without having to spend a dime. Also imagine that this productivity improvement is so simple that anyone can implement it starting today, with no costly training or certification programs required. Would you try it? Of course you would. You'd be crazy not to. It's called FRE: Frequent Recognition and Encouragement. Unfortunately, we don't often hear about this simple, no-cost, yet powerful way to engage employees.

Lean Six Sigma and other process-related productivity tools have taught us that to improve productivity, we must analyze, measure, and evaluate the *work*. We have come to believe that nothing is simple. Although we are certainly advocates of improving work processes, we also know that you can improve productivity by focusing on the *worker*, and we've got the data to prove it.

A CIO we work with was curious. He wanted to know why only some of his teams completed their projects on time and

EXCUSES, EXCUSES

We've heard just about all the excuses for why managers
don't offer frequent recognition and encouragement. Here
are the five most common ones:

- "I'm too busy."

- "That's what they get paid to do."

- "It's too early to celebrate. We haven't completely
  implemented this yet."

- "I don't like or need encouragement to do my job."

- "It'll go to their heads."

on budget, and seemed to enjoy their work more than others. In
particular, he wanted to know if teams were more engaged and productive when led by an optimistic manager. We conducted a study
to find out.

What was the secret ingredient? Optimism? No. It was FRE:
Frequent Recognition and Encouragement. Employees were given
a series of statements such as, "My project manager recognizes
my accomplishments regularly," and follow-up questions such as,
"How frequently and in what ways does your project manager offer
encouragement and/or recognize accomplishments?" Their answers
to those and other questions were then compared with the results
of the projects on which they worked. For example, how well did
those projects meet budget, schedule, and quality standards?

What Greenberg and Arakawa found was that managers who
provided frequent recognition and encouragement had significantly

higher project performance. Specifically, managers who scored in the top quartile for giving frequent recognition and encouragement saw a 42 percent increase in productivity compared with managers who scored in the bottom quartile.

Unfortunately, only 40 percent of the employees surveyed said they received any encouragement at all from their managers. It may surprise you that more managers don't use recognition and encouragement, but remember negativity bias. We are accustomed to look for what's wrong rather than what's right.

Let's find out how you would fare if you had participated in our study. Take the five-item FRE Manager Self-Assessment in Appendix D or on our website ProfitFromThePositive.com. Or simply consider how much you agree with this statement: "I regularly recognize the accomplishments of my employees."

But don't stop there because it really doesn't matter what you think you do. What really matters is what your employees experience. Ask your employees to take the FRE Employee Assessment of Manager in Appendix D or on our website and then compare their results with yours.

Think Process, Not Person

There is one more finding from positive psychology research that business leaders must know for FRE to be effective and not backfire. Although we rarely use the term *praise* in the business world, it's an important concept to understand. Research studies by Carol Dweck of Stanford University have found that process praise is more effective than person praise.

Person praise is when we recognize someone by using general statements such as, "You did a really good job," and, "You're really smart." Dweck and her colleagues have found that this kind of praise actually promotes helplessness and fear of losing the positive reputation if the person makes a mistake. *Process praise*, in comparison, is when we recognize someone by describing the effort or strategy he used to achieve the results by saying things such as, "I really appreciate the time and attention you put into analyzing those reports when I know you had a lot of other responsibilities." This kind of praise was found to promote more self-confidence and resilience in employees, especially when they were faced with future difficulties.

Lastly, feedback must be *genuine* to be received well. "My colleagues can vouch for my toughness," says Robert Eckert, who retired in 2012 as chairman of the world's largest toy company, Mattel. "But what's wrong with recognizing a job well done? Why not say thank you more often—and mean it?"

One way to be sure your feedback will be perceived as genuine is to stop whatever else you're doing and focus exclusively on your colleague. If you are fully present, the employee will pick up on your sincerity. If you lead people in other locations, you can convey your sincerity even over the phone. Again, stop whatever you're doing (yes, turn away from your computer screen) and focus all of your attention on the employee.

Many of the business leaders we work with are responsible for large multi-million-dollar projects that take years to fully implement. A question we often get from them is, "How can I recognize my team when it will take years to know if we're successful?"

Recognizing employees is neither difficult nor time-consuming, as demonstrated by our client Tatiana. Tatiana is the project manager for a multi-million-dollar systems conversion. Success would not be evident for at least two years. Should she have waited until the project was fully implemented before she recognized accomplishments? No. She provided frequent recognition and encouragement, using a variety of methods: in person at project team meetings, by leaving periodic group voice mails, and by forwarding emails from internal business partners who praised the team's progress. Bottom line? Don't let the only time your team hears from you be when something is wrong.

Stab in the Heart, Praise to the Back, and Other Things That Work

Keep in mind that FRE doesn't necessarily have to come only from you, the leader. Team members who regularly recognize each other's efforts can be equally motivating.

Christa Foley, senior manager of HR at Zappos University, told us, "Create programs that encourage recognition from managers to employees and peer to peer. The more recognition your employees get from various sources, the better. We have several recognition programs that are low cost and definitely high ROI from an engagement standpoint. For example, each month, any employee can give another employee a $50 bonus for WOWing them. . . . The bonus receiver's manager also gets an email letting them know what great thing their employee did, and lastly, all bonus info and winners are compiled and shared with the whole company."

EverFi, which you learned about in Chapter 1, is a big proponent of manager and peer-to-peer recognition. But it also has a very interesting philosophy when it comes to providing FRE. "Stab in the heart and praise to the back," EverFi's Tom Davidson told us. "We have a very frank conversation when we think one of our team members is not performing up to the standards we expect. We do it to their face or what I call stab in the heart. But we're also big believers in you build people up when their back is turned. It's easy to recognize one of your teammates publicly, and we do that on companywide calls, but what makes our culture unique is we are big cheerleaders behind people's backs."

One of our clients, Elliot, told us what a thrill it was when he received dozens of text messages one afternoon from colleagues around the company. "I wasn't able to attend the Town Hall meeting that day," he told us. "I had no idea the leader was going to single me out as an example of living one of our company values." Praise to the back will eventually reverberate back to the person who deserves the recognition.

Remember, FRE doesn't cost a dime and, if done right, can boost a team's performance by over 40 percent. "Our culture is based on the fact that people have an innate need for well-deserved recognition," says David C. Novak, chairman, CEO, and president of Yum! Brands, whose chains include KFC, Pizza Hut, Taco Bell, and Long John Silver's. "Using recognition is the best way to build a high-energy, fun culture and reinforce the behaviors that drive results. It needs to be deserved, and it needs to come from the heart. For the people who are getting it done, it can't be done too much. Why be selfish on the thing that matters most to people?" Don't be stingy!

KEY TAKEAWAYS

Creating a highly engaged workforce is about bringing out the best in others. More and more companies are recognizing productivity gains when they focus more on what people do naturally well rather than constantly focusing on what they do poorly. There are four concrete ways to engage your employees and bring out their best:

- **Don't just read the book.** Once you understand and embrace your own strengths, introduce strengths to your employees. But don't just have them read a book on how to use strengths. Instead, make strengths part of your conversations with employees and help them craft their jobs into work that truly energizes them.

- **Turn strengths into a team sport.** You can also introduce strengths to your own intact work team, cross-functional project teams, and business partners by facilitating a group discussion. Boost performance by leveraging the strengths of the people you work with.

- **Don't fire poor performers; fire 'em up.** Talk with your employees periodically about how well their strengths align with the work you are asking them to perform. If one of your employees is not performing well, rather than getting frustrated and "writing him up," coach him by using the flow model. Recraft the job to make it a better fit.

- **Give FRE: Frequent Recognition and Encouragement.** Top-down, formal recognition programs may have their place, but don't overlook the power of simply expressing your thanks for what your employees do. Be sure your feedback is specific by focusing on the process the employee used to achieve great results and always be genuine.

● ● ● **REFLECTION QUESTIONS** ● ● ●

After reading this chapter, ask yourself these questions:

1. What am I already doing right to bring out the best in my employees?

2. How will I go about introducing strengths to my employees? Individually? As part of a team meeting? As part of some other work we have to do together?

3. Are there people or teams in other parts of my company who need to hear about strengths?

4. Who on my team would benefit from a flow discussion?

5. What are three recent individual or team accomplishments, and how will I recognize them? In person? By phone? Through an email? In a team meeting? Behind their back?

6. What is one small change I can make that will encourage my employees to perform their very best?

Performance Reviews:
Change 'Em or Chuck 'Em

We're not sure who dreads performance reviews more: the manager, the employee, or HR. We've had all three tell us that the preparation and subsequent discussions can be downright painful for four main reasons: we think they're a chore, we're stuck in a bad cycle, we artificially rank people, and we amplify shortcomings.

We think they're a chore. "My manager emailed me our company's performance review form," our client Michelle told us.

"What kind of discussion did you have?" we asked.

"Discussion?" Michelle seemed perplexed. "Our 'discussion' consisted of a half a dozen words in an email: 'Fill it out. I'll sign it.'"

Some managers perceive performance reviews as a dreaded check-off-the-box chore whose only purpose is to satisfy the human resources department. HR often inadvertently reinforces this perspective by focusing manager training on how to fill out the online forms rather than on how to have a constructive conversation.

Consequently, some managers fail to see the connection between investing time with employees to discuss performance and development plans and how this dialogue can result in increased productivity and engagement. Some employees view the process as a chore, too, if in the past they worked for managers who truly didn't care about their development and told them so.

We're stuck in a bad cycle. The thought of conducting performance reviews before year end for his 12 direct reports had our client, Max, in a knot. "Between my own deliverables and the year-end close I'm swamped," says Max. "I really do want to have a productive conversation with each of my directs, but I don't have the time to gather the necessary feedback, write up a review, and schedule 12 one-hour meetings."

In many companies, as in Max's, performance reviews and development discussions occur only once or maybe twice a year. Tight year-end deadlines (not to mention holidayitis when the annual cycle typically falls in December) leave little time to do the preparation that's needed to have a meaningful discussion. What happens instead is that the conversation between the manager and the employee is forced, inconvenient, and rushed, if it happens at all.

We artificially rank people. Many organizations continue to require their managers to use a stack ranking system when they are evaluating employee performance. Say you manage a 10-member team. Although most if not all may be high performers, it doesn't matter. You can only give two employees an "excellent" rating, three a "strong" rating, and three more a "solid" rating, and two must receive a "needs improvement" rating (which is a euphemism for "you'd better shape up or you'll be out the door").

"The bell curve system really represented a glass half empty mentality," says Peter McDonald, VP of human resources at Unum, a leading disability insurer. "When it came to the 'needs improvement' people, all of the good stuff the employee did was missed or deemphasized. It became a self-fulfilling prophecy. The people who got the 'excellent' and 'strong' ratings got a lot of grooming, positive feedback, and plum assignments."

Imagine you're an employee who has worked hard all year only to find out during your annual performance review that you can't be given the highest rating because of some arbitrary archaic system. What do you think that might do to your level of engagement? At one Fortune 100 technology company, employees, both current and former, who were interviewed for an article cited stack ranking as "the most destructive process . . . something that drove out untold numbers of employees." Even HR leaders who manage the overall process believe the system is broken. In a 2012 study by the Society of Human Resource Management, 45 percent of HR leaders believed that the annual performance review is not an accurate assessment of employee performance.

We amplify shortcomings. "I had more positive feedback than negative," says our client Ken, referring to a performance review he had with one of his employees last year that still haunts him. "No matter how I tried to guide the discussion back to her accomplishments, she obsessed over the one place I thought she could improve."

"My manager spent the first few minutes highlighting what I did well over the last year," says Sean, a business analyst for a large healthcare insurer. "But then he spent the rest of my performance review nitpicking over things that happened months ago."

Rather than feeling pumped up to do an even better job, Sean left the meeting feeling deflated and demotivated.

Again, negativity bias, which you learned about in Chapter 4, is often alive and well during performance review time. Many managers and employees alike discount or deemphasize accomplishments and instead focus on shortcomings.

Negativity bias also rears its ugly head when the review moves into a discussion of where the employee needs to develop. We didn't have to look far for a real-life example.

Margaret worked in the training and development department of a large financial services company. Every year she received accolades from her internal customers on how the team-building sessions she designed and facilitated boosted their results. Yet every year in her development plan, the following sentence would appear: "Margaret would benefit by enrolling in the course 'Fundamentals of the Insurance Industry Financials.'"

"I already possessed a good working knowledge of the businesses I supported," says Margaret. "The very thought of sitting through a two-hour course for six consecutive weeks made me break into a cold sweat. I successfully dodged this energy-draining bullet for three performance review cycles."

Margaret's manager, like so many managers even today, could not understand that her development could consist of anything other than filling a gap. She couldn't see how both the company and Margaret could benefit if she furthered developed her strengths: learning more about building teams. What ultimately happened?

Margaret left the company and started her own consulting practice. More than 16 years later, she continues to consult for the financial services industry and "Fundamentals of the Insurance Industry Financials" has become a moot point.

Think Energize, Not Evaluate

We often believe that the main purpose of performance reviews is to evaluate performance. What we often lose sight of is that performance reviews can provide a wonderful opportunity to energize a team for the coming year. Think energize, not evaluate! Unfortunately, these conversations can backfire. Employees often walk away from performance reviews feeling anything but energized, and managers often walk away feeling frustrated. Many innovative companies have already given performance reviews the boot. Performance reviews "mostly suck," says Robert Sutton, a Stanford University management professor. "If you have regular conversations with people and they know where they stand, then the performance evaluation is maybe unnecessary."

In this chapter we show you four findings from positive psychology research so that you can turn these annual powwows into meaningful conversations: obsess over strengths but don't ignore weaknesses; don't make goals easy and vague; preview, don't just review, performance; and chew the fat, don't chew them out.

1. OBSESS OVER STRENGTHS BUT DON'T IGNORE WEAKNESSES

When it comes to performance and development planning discussions, most plans are still built around "areas of opportunity," a euphemism for "weaknesses," and most training dollars continue to be spent on plugging gaps in people's performance. We don't want you to think we're antidevelopment. If there are clearly derailers in an employee's career or skills he needs to improve or acquire to perform his current job well or prepare him for future roles, these should be addressed through training, coaching, or mentoring. But imagine if a manager asked an employee how she might use her strengths to further her development. In a Corporate Leadership Council study of over 20,000 employees in 29 countries, researchers found that focusing on employee strengths during reviews led to a 36 percent improvement in performance.

Clearly, a manager's role is to help employees improve performance and continue to grow and develop in their careers. We are not advocating that you skip over or ignore weaknesses. In fact, NYU Stern School of Business professor Jonathan Haidt wanted to find out if there were any differences between people who engaged in activities to build on their strengths and those who took on activities to shore up their weaknesses. The positive psychology community was surprised when Haidt found that those working on strengths did not report any additional physical, mental, or emotional health benefits over those working on weaknesses. The only difference he found was that working on strengths was more *enjoyable* than working on weaknesses.

In short, weaknesses that are important to one's success should still be addressed in the workplace and in one's life. What we are advocating is spending more time discussing what your employees have done well and how they can use their strengths in new and different ways in the weeks and months ahead.

"Margaret conducted her research study here at The Hanover and found that managers who pay more attention to employees' strengths achieve higher levels of team performance," says Greg Tranter, EVP, CIO, and COO. "As a result of that study we have since changed our performance management process to include much more emphasis on the leveraging of strengths in our employees' development plans."

Speak the Same Language

In Chapter 6 we showed you how to help your employees uncover their strengths. Now you can keep their strengths top of mind by using the actual strengths language when writing their reviews. One of our clients, Carolyn, did just that when she wrote a review for her project leader Ann using the language from *StrengthsFinder 2.0*. Notice how she uses strengths to highlight both what Ann has accomplished and where she needs to develop in the months ahead:

> Ann, you give new meaning to the ACHIEVER strength: you consistently stay focused, work hard and deliver on all promises, often ahead of schedule. You are STRATEGIC and are energized by learning new things (LEARNER). You excel in your horizontal project leader role and you have brought well thought out ideas to the table on how to deliver the most to the business. Keep leveraging your LEARNER strength to broaden your knowledge of the new business processes.

Don't skip over weaknesses but don't obsess over them either. If one of your employees has a tendency to skip right over what he has done well and zero in on weaknesses, slow him down. Be sure he truly acknowledges his strengths and what he has accomplished.

Don't Outsource, Crowdsource

Finally, don't forget to solicit feedback from coworkers, business partners, and customers to get a clearer picture of an employee's accomplishments, strengths, and areas where she could improve. "Crowdsource your performance reviews," says Eric Mosley, CEO and cofounder of Globoforce and coauthor of *Winning with a Culture of Recognition.* Crowdsourcing borrows from research on the wisdom of crowds. The bottom line? "A group of independently deciding individuals is more likely to make better decisions and more accurate observations than is an individual."

Some companies, such as Firefox developer Mozilla and Great Harvest Bread Company, are using social-media-type programs to gather real-time feedback on how employees are performing against goals. If you are ready to jump into crowdsourcing feedback, there are innovative companies that will collect online feedback that could make the annual performance review obsolete.

Although the very term *performance review* conjures up an assessment of the past, it is also a good time to discuss the future. In this next tool we look at one place where goals make sense and why you should make them difficult to achieve.

2. DON'T MAKE GOALS EASY AND VAGUE

After reading Chapter 1, you know that creating positive habits and routines can beat just setting goals. Remember "same time, same place"? You'll achieve your goals faster if you turn them into habits. But that assumes that you've set a goal to begin with. Move beyond reviewing an employee's performance. Use this time to set some new goals. But how?

In Chapter 6 we learned why *specific* feedback does more to bring out an employee's best than does more *general* feedback such as "great job." The notion of specificity also applies to how best to set and achieve goals for the months or year ahead. Difficult and specific goals lead to significantly higher performance than do easy or vague goals or no goals at all. When we set difficult goals, maximum effort kicks in. In business we often call these *stretch* goals.

"Challenging goals facilitate pride in accomplishment," says goals researcher Gary Latham of the University of Toronto's Rotman School of Management. In study after study of occupations ranging from loggers to engineers with similar abilities, those who set challenging and specific goals performed better than those who didn't.

One of our clients, Lisa, came to a coaching call one day frustrated that her operations manager was not meeting her expectations: "It's already the end of February, and we're way behind schedule. I thought we would have at least two offices converted by now. It's really impacting service levels."

"What was his goal?" we inquired.

"We agreed at the beginning of the year that the new process would be implemented in all field offices by June 1 and that that would include training staff, too."

We coached Lisa on how she could work with her operations manager to develop a more specific goal with biweekly milestones.

Remember, when goals are vague, such as telling employees to "just do your best," we inadvertently lower their effort. When we create specific goals together, an employee knows what effective performance looks like, and that will make your job of providing constructive feedback later on much easier.

When "Do Your Best" Works

When employees are *learning* a new job or task, asking them to do their best results in higher performance than does setting a specific and challenging goal. This is the case because fear of failure is minimized when we tell ourselves we're just going to put forth our best effort when learning a new task. Remember the learner mindset in Chapter 2?

Setting specific goals that are difficult to achieve is an exercise in looking ahead. You can apply this future orientation to change the dreaded performance review. How? Read on.

3. PREVIEW, DON'T JUST REVIEW, PERFORMANCE

Performance reviews, as the name suggests, have traditionally been the time when we look back on what an employee has achieved. However, imagine using performance reviews to also *preview* performance and set up the conditions for a successful year ahead. Professional athletes have been applying this preview or mental rehearsing technique for years.

Sports psychologists train athletes to visualize a successful game, match, race, or swing. You can apply the same practices with your employees. Here's how:

We know from traditional psychology that writing about past traumatic events can help people overcome their negative experiences. We also know from positive psychology that writing about what you hope to accomplish in the future can be a powerful tool for increasing happiness and life satisfaction. University of Missouri psychologist Laura King has found that writing about what you hope to accomplish boosts positive feelings about the future, increases your belief in yourself, and leads to self-fulfilling prophecies.

Performance ~~Re~~Previews

Imagine if we asked employees to write their goals for the upcoming year from the perspective that they had already attained them. That's what our client Kathy Owen, chief information officer at Unum, did:

"Goals are typically vague and written in generalities. I decided to ask each employee to write their goals from this future perspective: 'Imagine that it is a year from now and you are writing your performance review. What would you have to say about what you accomplished?' What people came back with was amazing."

However, visualizing success is not enough. You must also ask your employees to visualize *how* they will achieve even greater performance next year. Before midterm exams, University of California, Los Angeles, psychologists Shelley Taylor and Lien Pham asked college students to visualize either the *process* for doing well on an exam (good study habits) or the desired *outcome* (getting a good grade). The students who imagined the process they would use actually performed better on the exam than did those who only imagined getting a good grade. Therefore, don't just ask your employees to visualize and write about their goals and accomplishments from this future perspective; also ask them to describe what specifically they would have done to achieve such a positive review.

Unfortunately, performance reviews can still create a lot of angst for managers and employees alike. They can feel like a big, heavy annual career-altering event. But it doesn't have to be that way if you treat performance reviews like any other thoughtful conversation you might have.

4. CHEW THE FAT; DON'T CHEW THEM OUT

You can take the angst out of performance reviews by reframing the way you perceive them. Rather than thinking the meeting is something you must *conduct*, view it as just another conversation. If you talk about performance on a regular basis with employees, the midyear or year-end review should simply be a recap of what you have already discussed. Frequent feedback has been shown over and over to be more effective than less frequent feedback. How often you should give it—daily, weekly, monthly, or quarterly—can be determined simply by assessing the employee's level of experience versus the level of challenge the goal presents. The higher the challenge and the lower an employee's experience is, the more frequent your feedback should be. Remember the flow model we introduced you to in Chapter 6? The same principle applies.

Surprises Not Welcome

Some companies we work with have a "no surprise" rule, meaning that the manager cannot raise any performance issues at the year-end-review that haven't already been discussed with the employee. This policy makes it clear that the manager is responsible for addressing issues as they arise rather than waiting for a formal performance review to ding the employee.

One of the most common questions we get from our clients is, "How can I deliver tough performance feedback without damaging morale?" Delivering tough performance feedback isn't easy even for the most skilled among us because we're never quite sure how a person will receive it.

One of Landon's employees, Grace, is a good performer but not what he would call a team player. She gets her own work done, but in the peer feedback Landon collected he learned that she doesn't offer to help her teammates when they have questions. Landon has a quarterly review with Grace coming up. He's concerned that if he brings up the matter, Grace will get defensive. We coached Landon on how to turn the review into a conversation:

"Grace, I'm really impressed with the quality and timeliness of your work. I continue to receive positive feedback from your internal customers on how quickly you turn around their requests. You are one of the most experienced people on this team, and there is a lot others could learn from you if you made yourself more available to them. Our two newest employees, Kevin and Akia, would really benefit if you shared your extensive knowledge of our system."

Landon went on to explain that having more knowledge of the system would give the two new employees the confidence they needed to answer customers' questions and not have to interrupt him as much with their own questions: "Imagine if Kevin and Akia could handle 95 percent of the calls themselves."

At first Grace resisted: "I am so busy with my own work that I don't have time to help them."

That was when Landon became curious: "Well, what *could* you do without negatively impacting your own work?"

"I could try spending 30 minutes every Friday morning, when we know our call volume is the lowest, and review our most common customer inquiries with both of them."

"I bet within four weeks you could build Kevin and Akia's knowledge so they could handle most calls themselves."

Rather than chewing Grace out for not helping her coworkers, Landon had a conversation with her instead. Two weeks later, Landon made a point of recognizing Grace's efforts to help the team:

"Grace, I've noticed in the last two weeks that Kevin and Akia are only coming to me once or twice a day for customer questions. Tell me, what do you notice? What else do you think they need to learn? How can you help them?"

Landon had successfully delivered tough performance feedback without damaging morale. The added benefit? Grace, Kevin, and Akia were behaving more like a team.

KEY TAKEAWAYS

Performance reviews don't have to be something you and your employees dread. Reframe the way you perceive performance reviews. Think of performance reviews as a time to reenergize, not evaluate, your employees. Specifically, do the following:

- **Obsess over strengths but don't ignore weaknesses.** Use the language of strengths when writing and talking about performance. Be sure to identify ways your employees can develop their strengths even more. Remember, don't ignore weaknesses, but don't focus all of your time there.

- **Don't make goals easy and vague.** Regardless of whether goals are set by the employee, assigned by you, or set together in a more participative way, specific and challenging goals motivate people to perform. Remember, people will rise to our expectations. Review goals periodically, not once a year.

- **Preview, don't just review, performance.** Ask your employees to not only review their performance but preview it for the year ahead. Have them imagine that it is a year from now and you're meeting to discuss how well they performed. Ask them to visualize what a successful year would have looked like and what specifically they would have done to accomplish it. Make it stick by having your employees not only think about next year's success but write about it too.

- **Chew the fat; don't chew them out.** Don't "conduct" a performance review. Make it a conversation instead.

Like great sports coaches, business leaders have more influence over how well people perform than they may realize. Change the annual performance review into more frequent and meaningful conversations or get rid of it altogether. Visit our website Profit FromThePositive.com for more information on how to prepare for a performance review.

● ● ● REFLECTION QUESTIONS ● ● ●

After reading this chapter, ask yourself these questions:

1. What am I already doing right when it comes to reviewing performance and energizing employees?

2. How often should I be meeting with employees to discuss their performance and development plans?

3. Who have I been avoiding delivering tough performance feedback to? What's a better way to approach this employee?

4. In preparing for a performance discussion, how do I collect feedback today, and what else should I do going forward?

5. What's one new approach I'll use to set goals for this year?

6. How can I influence the HR practices at my company?

7. What is one small change I can make in the way I deliver performance feedback and energize my employees?

Meetings:
From Energy Buster to
Energy Booster

"I practically live in meetings. From the time I arrive in the morning until the time I leave, I am in back-to-back meetings. Sometimes I'm double- and triple-booked. I never have time to just think," says our client Gloria, the vice president of application development at a Fortune 200 company.

Gloria is responsible for delivering high-quality IT projects on time and on budget. She and her team must work closely with business analysts, programmers, and architects to implement solutions for her customers. Consequently, she leads and participates in a lot of meetings. If Gloria has 10 people attend an hourlong meeting, that's 10 hours that could have been spent reducing backlog, serving customers, moving a project forward, or developing the next product.

Having worked in and consulted to dozens of organizations, we've often seen three problems with meetings: we have too many, they are unproductive, and participation is off.

We have too many. How many meetings or calls did you have today? One account suggests that every day there are 11 million meetings in the United States. A Fortune 100 healthcare company that we work with reports a total of 350,000 hours spent in audio conferences. You might be thinking this number of hours annually isn't so bad because it is a large company, but in fact, 350,000 hours worth of meetings occurred in just one month. This particular company was encouraging employees to take the "10 percent challenge" to reduce time spent in meetings.

The National Statistics Council reports that people spend 37 percent of their time in meetings. Another report calculates meeting time by the size of the company: managers at large companies spend up to 75 percent of their total time preparing for, attending, and following up on meetings, whereas managers at small companies spend about 10 percent of their time.

They're unproductive. Many meetings are not productive and, because of the number of hours they consume, can be quite costly. Two groups of researchers measured the effectiveness of meetings: one group measured effectiveness in terms of time, and the other measured it in terms of cost. The first group found that 50 percent of meeting time is wasted. The second group translated time lost to meetings into about $37 billion annually in the United States alone. These are big numbers, and what do they say? Streamlining, overhauling, or eliminating meetings altogether could save your company a bundle. One of the problems is that 60 minutes is an artificial and standard length that is rarely questioned. But there is no evidence that 1-hour meetings are any more effective than meetings that are 15, 30, or 45 minutes in length.

Another problem is that decisions rarely are made in meetings. We talk and talk and talk some more, and then the meeting ends abruptly when the clock strikes the hour. Usually the participants are eager to get to their next meeting, leaving little time to clarify decisions or next steps or to gain a commitment to move forward. Unfortunately, we have to agree with Aesop when it comes to the ineffectiveness of most meetings: After all is said and done, more is said than done.

Participation is off. "Some of our meetings turn into gripe sessions," Gloria went on to explain. "Of course some of our meetings are more productive than others, but sometimes it is like pulling teeth to get people to contribute."

A lot of meetings are conducted for meet-and-disburse-information purposes. In those cases, email might be a better medium. But when we do bring people together, participation is often limited to a few extroverted types. We also tend to assume that if everyone is physically present, all the attendees must be attentive and actively listening. Wrong. If people are not participating, their minds wander (and so do their fingertips on their laptops). When meetings are by conference call, participation can be even lower. Remember what our client Eddie in Chapter 1 was doing while his phone was on mute?

Regardless of your profession, a good portion of your workweek is spent preparing for, attending, or leading meetings. Consequently, we would be remiss if we didn't offer some practical, no-cost ways to improve them. We're going to assume that you have or will take an inventory of your meetings and shorten, eliminate, or send a substitute when that is possible. We're also going to assume that you already apply sound practices to your meetings, such as providing an agenda and relevant materials in advance, starting and stopping on time, and capturing and communicating key actions steps or decisions after the meeting. What else can you do?

In this chapter, you will learn ways to stop the meeting madness that eats away at not only your time and money but also your energy. First, avoid having your next meeting turn into a gripe session by using the magic ratio. Second, learn how to apply the peak-end rule to boost the energy in your next meeting. Third, learn how to play your whole bench.

1. START WITH A SIZZLE

It's unrealistic to assume that everyone assembled around the table or calling in for the meeting is in a good mood, focused, and applying his or her best thinking to your agenda. In fact, 91 percent of attendees admit to daydreaming during meetings. Additionally, they may have just gotten off the phone with an irate customer, sat through three boring back-to-back meetings, or be preoccupied with a pressing problem.

The way you start your meetings does indeed matter. We all know about icebreakers: the exercises facilitators sometimes make us do to get acquainted with one another. But what you probably don't know is that starting a meeting on a positive note can actually bring out your team's best thinking. University of North Carolina psychologist Barbara Fredrickson has found that positive emotions such as enthusiasm and interest serve two functions: they broaden our perspective and build psychological capital.

Banking on Psychological Capital

Just as businesses have inventory and physical capital, people have psychological capital. This refers to the emotional reserves people use to deal with difficult situations. This concept is part of Fredrickson's *broaden-and-build theory* of positive emotions. Psychologists have been studying negative emotions such as anger, sadness, and fear for decades, but only in the last decade or so have they studied positive emotions. What Fredrickson found is that people routinely build up psychological capital through positive emotional experiences such as receiving recognition for a job well done or talking about their accomplishments. When we are in a good mood, we are more open to possibilities, more creative, and full of an internal reservoir of energy that we can draw on when the going gets tough.

Another researcher, Marcial Losada, has found that high-performing teams differ from low-performing teams in their ratio of positive to negative comments. Losada and his researchers observed 60 business teams in strategic planning meetings. The researchers tracked the words used by the team members, coding them as either supportive or critical, to come up with a ratio for each team.

Losada wanted to know if there was any connection between a team's ratio of positive to negative comments and the results that team achieved. What he found was that the highest-performing teams had a ratio of positive to negative of about 3:1—three positive emotions expressed for every negative emotion. Think about your last team meeting. What was the positive-to-negative ratio?

If you are highly intuitive, you probably can sense the mood in a meeting—positive or negative. If you're more analytical, at your next meeting take a piece of paper and draw a line down the middle. Label one side "Positive" and the other "Negative." Make tick marks in the appropriate column as each person contributes. If the discussion is tilting toward the negative, intervene at the next natural break in the conversation.

STAY IN THE ZONE

The *Losada Zone* is a concept that refers to a healthy interpersonal relationship in which the ratio of positive to negative interactions is between 3:1 and 12:1. What happens when people give fewer than three positive comments for each negative? It feels lousy, and the reason is that you feel criticized. The relationship can become dysfunctional. In contrast, what tends to happen when the ratio is higher than 12 positives to each negative comment? It feels superficial because people are likely avoiding conflict. The relationship can also appear phony.

There's No Magic in the Magic Ratio

There are a number of ways to start meetings with a sizzle. You can ask a positive question, recognize an individual or team effort, or tell a funny or interesting story. An objection we hear when we propose such ideas to clients is, "How can we do that without eating up valuable time?" It's easy. Before you dive into an agenda, even one full of challenges, take a few minutes to ask a positive question or pose a positive prompt. Keep in mind that not everyone has to share his or her answer out loud. In fact, if everyone did that, it would probably take up too much time. Finally, take the pressure off yourself and tap into your team's creativity by rotating who comes up with the prompt.

Our client Hunter, who heads a finance team at a Fortune 100 company, began his weekly staff meeting with, "Tell me the best thing that's happened to you since we met last week." The effect this prompt had on the team was contagious. By the time two or three people had shared their responses, the other team members who had walked into the meeting feeling harried had caught the positive vibe (remember the contagion effect from Chapter 3?).

Many leaders, especially those in technical fields such as finance, IT, and engineering, are often skeptical about beginning a meeting with a positive question. Try it a couple of times and notice what happens to your team's energy.

However, meetings don't always go the way we think they will. In fact, sometimes they get off on the wrong foot, even for professional facilitators like us. Margaret was working with an IT team that had been charged with implementing a multi-million-dollar system. Seeking a positive start to the meeting, she kicked off the session by asking the team to reflect on the last six months: "What have you accomplished since I last worked with you?"

This prompt did not go as Margaret planned. The first team member began, "I guess we did okay." The next member said with an air of disappointment, "There's definitely a need for improvement and efficiency." The next three people went on to explain some of the delays in the project. The positive energy that had been present over coffee before the meeting had drained out of the room like a popped balloon.

Then the sixth team member said: "Considering the magnitude of this project and our challenges, we still delivered a lot." He went on to cite what the team had accomplished.

Margaret decided that this was an opportunity to try a different approach: "I suggest that we take a brief detour so I can introduce a new concept that I think will help us have a more productive discussion today." She explained the 3:1 ratio and continued, "What we experienced in the last 10 minutes was a 1:5 ratio—one positive to five negatives. I'm not here to shut down the critiques, but I want to be sure we highlight what's gone right, too. Can we have a redo?"

What Gifts and Music Can Do

Another way to improve people's moods and make them more effective problem solvers is to offer them a small gift. In one study, three sets of doctors were asked to make a complex liver diagnosis. Before giving their diagnoses, one group was asked to read the medical profession's ethical code. The second group was given a small token of appreciation to enjoy later (a piece of candy). The third group wasn't asked or given anything before its diagnoses. What happened? The liver diagnoses of the doctors who had been given the small gift were three times more accurate.

So what? Giving people a small gift puts them into a good mood, which in turn actually improves people's ability to solve problems. Hand out a healthy snack or an inexpensive gift (it can be as simple as an interesting quote on an index card) at the start of your meetings and notice what happens. But let's be realistic. Chances are that you're not going to offer a small gift at every meeting you hold. Pick and choose the spots where a small gift will be most helpful.

Additionally, the positive psychological effects of music, such as improving one's mood and reducing fatigue, have been well documented in both sports and fitness. The same benefits can be applied in meetings. Music is particularly effective for large group meetings in which it takes some time to get people seated. Play some upbeat music as people enter the room. When the music stops, that cues the group that the meeting is about to start. Use music over breaks and at the end of meetings, too.

Now that you know how to start your meetings with a sizzle, it is equally important not to let meetings fizzle out at the end.

2. PRACTICE THE PEAK-END RULE

Daniel Kahneman, Princeton University psychologist and Nobel Prize winner, ran a series of studies to learn how people evaluate past experiences. Kahneman and his colleagues found that people use a mental shortcut to recall events. People average the peak experience and the end experience to come up with their remembered experience. Psychologists call this the *peak-end rule*, and it is illustrated in the following chart. Here's how it works:

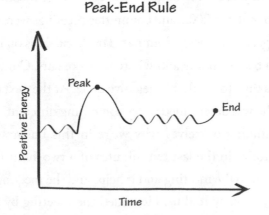

Peak-End Rule

Suppose you and a colleague attended a two-day conference. You both listened to a leading expert speak on a topic you were both eager to learn more about (the peak). However, on the last day, you each picked a different breakout session to attend (the end). Yours was disappointing. The speaker was boring, and the content had little relevance to your business. By contrast, the final breakout session your colleague attended was led by a lively speaker, and the information was pertinent to her business. When people ask, "How was the conference?" you give a tepid response and your colleague gives a glowing account.

Let's apply the peak-end rule to how you can get the most out of your meetings. You probably have a natural peak: some point when the energy is highest. You can create an upbeat ending that will motivate people to take action by applying the same techniques you used in starting your meetings, such as asking a positive question.

Again, our clients are often skeptical at first: "How can I possibly end a meeting on a positive note when people are rushing off to their next meeting?"

Let's see how Chip Conley, whom you met in Chapter 2, transformed Joie de Vivre's executive committee meetings at their darkest hour. It was 2002, and committee meetings were downright depressing. Agendas were dominated by discussions on how to stay afloat in a bad economy and where to make cuts. Conley decided that it was time to break this negative cycle. At the next committee meeting, he was determined to try something different.

"Reminding ourselves why we're in this business, let's tell positive stories in the last ten minutes of a two-hour meeting. It doesn't cut into the meeting and it helps end the meeting on a positive note," Conley told us. He ended the meeting by telling the story of a hotel employee who had gone above and beyond requirements and had done something wonderful for a guest. The following day, three managers told similar stories. The snowball effect had taken over.

ENDINGS MATTER: QUESTIONS TO WRAP UP YOUR MEETINGS

Don't let your meetings fizzle. Put the peak-end rule into practice by asking questions like these:

- What did you find most useful or valuable?

- What are you taking away that you are most excited about?

- Who in the company do we want to give a hats-off to?

Now that you know how to start meetings with a sizzle and make sure they don't fizzle, here's one more tool to transform your meetings from an energy buster to an energy booster.

3. PLAY YOUR WHOLE BENCH

An overwhelming majority of meeting attendees (92 percent) believe that meetings have the potential to be a wonderful place to contribute. So why do meetings typically fall short? Maybe you're not encouraging or expecting every member of your team to contribute. Let's see how you can play your whole bench at your next meeting.

Remember Losada, who came up with the magic ratio? In the same research he found another factor that drives team performance. He discovered that high-performing teams had a 1:1 ratio between how many *questions* they asked and how much *information* they shared.

Think of the meetings you attended this week. Were any of them dominated by people who only asked questions? Or maybe you were in a meeting dominated by people who were simply waiting for their turn to talk. Or, worse yet, the meeting leader or a particular team member just droned on and on. Chances are those meetings were unproductive.

What you want to strive for is a 1:1 ratio between asking questions and making a point. Therefore, be sure to play your whole bench and track participation until you and your team get the hang of it.

Getting people to speak up or shut up can be a challenge for any meeting facilitator, but it can be especially difficult when some or all members of your team are remote and you must rely on video or conference calls. What can you do? Before the meeting, on a sheet of paper, draw a circle representing a conference table—real or virtual. Draw circles around the table representing the people attending the meeting, including those on the phone, as in the drawing on the next page. Label each circle with a participant's name or initials. As each person contributes, put a mark next to his or her name. If someone constantly interrupts, acknowledge his point and then move on and solicit another perspective.

"We were 20 minutes into the meeting and I had only heard from the same two people again and again and virtually nothing from the others," said our client Patricia, the CEO of an early-stage medical devices company.

Track Participation

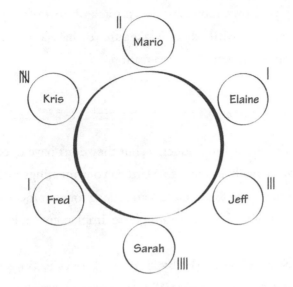

She suspected that the remote attendees had their phones on mute and were probably catching up on email. Patricia needed the full participation of her team members to be sure they were tackling the right priorities between now and year end. "What can I do to get everyone to participate?" Patricia asked us.

"Simply make balanced participation an explicit meeting norm," we advised. "Tell everyone you don't need superstars; you want to play your whole team. Then keep a scorecard to track participation until it becomes natural."

A Final Note on Meetings

When you're the meeting leader, it's much easier to implement the last three tips. However, many times you're a participant in someone else's meeting, maybe that of your boss or business partner. What can you do in that case?

Keep your own scorecard. Keep track of how often you contribute compared with others. Make sure you have a voice at the table yet don't dominate the conversation.

KEY TAKEAWAYS

Many meetings are unproductive, but they don't have to be. Imagine people actually looking forward to your meetings rather than dreading them. On top of having an agenda for your meeting, boost productivity with these three simple-to-implement tools:

- **Start with a sizzle.** By kicking off your meetings with a positive opener, you will increase your team's creativity and innovation. Ask a positive question, recognize an accomplishment, acknowledge a specific team success, tell an interesting or funny story, or offer a small gift. Remember, high-performing teams have a 3:1 magic ratio: three positives for every negative.

- **Practice the peak-end rule.** Don't let your meetings fizzle. People remember endings. Build time into your agenda to wrap up, reiterate next steps, and end on a positive note.

- **Play your whole bench.** Pay particular attention to how much questioning versus sharing information occurs in your meetings. Remember, high-performing teams also have a 1:1 ratio: a balance between asking questions and providing input.

Whether your meetings are conducted in person, by phone, or over the web, these practical tools apply. In fact, paying attention to the way you start and end a meeting and tracking participation may be even more important in virtual settings since you don't have the benefit of immediate and direct feedback.

● ● ● **REFLECTION QUESTIONS** ● ● ●

After reading this chapter, ask yourself these questions:

1. What am I already doing right to run productive meetings?

2. How would I rate my own PNR (positive-to-negative ratio) today?

3. What can I do to draw out the quieter members of my team?

4. Are there any meetings I could reduce in length or frequency or eliminate altogether?

5. How could I start and end the next meeting I'm leading on a more positive note?

6. In which meetings would I consider offering a small gift?

7. What can I do to positively influence meetings in which I am not the leader?

8. What is one small change I can implement that will make my meetings more effective?

PART III

Putting
It
All
Together

By now, we have given you over two dozen tools to boost productivity and transform your business. You've probably already put some of them into practice. In this last section, we weave together everything about you as the leader from Part I and everything about leading your team from Part II. But let's be honest. As you begin to implement the content in *Profit from the Positive*, you may run into some resistance. In this final section, we show you what our clients have done to overcome resistance and profit from the positive.

After reading this section, you will be able to:

- **Take action in the face of resistance.** For example, did you know that you are more likely to make progress if you start small?

- **Explain key concepts in simple terms.** For example, did you know that you don't ever have to utter the words *positive psychology* if you don't want to?

- **Start implementing these tools today.** For example, did you know that you don't have to go through any red tape to begin applying *Profit from the Positive* to your team or business?

THE POSITIVE DEVIANT:
No Budget? No Problem

Profit from the Positive began as a desire to share what's working with a much broader global audience. We've coached hundreds of executives, business owners, managers, and their teams by introducing them to the tools we've shared with you in *Profit from the Positive*. It has truly been a pleasure to watch our clients grow and transform their businesses by bringing these cutting-edge practices to their companies.

Let's talk for a moment about positive deviance. Imagine a bell curve of all the possible actions you could take (see the drawing on the next page). Now think of the positive long tail of that bell curve. Our 27 tools are those actions, and our clients became positive deviants when they took the leap to lead themselves and their businesses in this way.

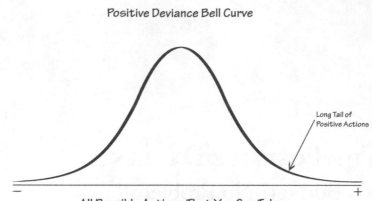

Positive Deviance Bell Curve

Long Tail of Positive Actions

−   +

All Possible Actions That You Can Take

We've learned four important lessons from our positive deviants that we want to pass along to you: don't resist resistance, start small, drop the lingo, and use the back door.

1. DON'T RESIST RESISTANCE

When we try to introduce something new, whether at work, at home, or in our community, our ideas are sometimes met with resistance. Naysayers and skeptics are everywhere; remember negativity bias? However, both our clients and we believe that resistance is a promising sign of change. When the people in our lives resist our ideas, it typically means that their pain points need to be addressed. Don't resist resistance; be empathic and address it. If you need some help explaining the concepts in *Profit from the Positive*, see Appendix E: The Five FRESH Themes: *f*it, *r*ight, *e*motions, *s*cience, and *h*abits.

Remember, not everyone will resist your ideas. Most likely you'll have some supporters too, in which case we recommend that you start small.

2. START SMALL

If you see yourself as a *Profit from the Positive* pioneer, chances are that your company's practices and other processes haven't quite caught up with you yet. For example, leadership development programs and performance reviews may still be built around closing gaps rather than leveraging strengths. Formal recognition programs for high performers and a progressive discipline policy for poor performers may still be the order of day rather than informal recognition and coaching to higher performance. Hiring practices may still favor technical skills over interpersonal skills and company fit. Strategy and business planning discussions may still employ the traditional SWOT analysis (strengths, weaknesses, opportunities, and threats) rather than a SOAR analysis (strengths, opportunities, aspirations, and results). Let's not forget that many business meetings may still be painfully boring, unproductive, and costly. Rather than trying to completely overhaul these business practices all at once, make small changes.

Where to Begin

In *Profit from the Positive*, you were introduced to well over two dozen tools to improve your personal and team productivity and your company's profits. That's a lot of tools in your toolbox. Instead of trying to implement all of them at once, focus on only three. Why only three? Because less is truly more.

Goals researchers have found that people are more likely to achieve their goals when they break them into smaller subgoals or discrete steps. Researchers have found that subgoals build people's

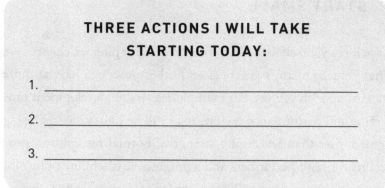

confidence, making them more likely to take on bigger challenges in the future.

As you recall, at the end of each of the previous eight chapters we asked you several reflection questions. The last question was always: What is one small change I can make? If you jotted down your answer to this question, go back to the end of each chapter and reread what you wrote. In the space above, write down three small changes you will make today. Yes, only three. If you didn't jot down your answers, use the space to list your three small changes (for a refresher on all the tools, see Appendix A).

3. DROP THE LINGO

A sure way to turn people off from your ideas is to sound like a brainiac, flinging around jargon no one is familiar with. Positive psychology? Who cares? You don't ever need to utter those two words if you don't want to. Instead, spend at least part of your workweek looking for things that are going right. Gollwitzer's study? Who cares? Instead, coach your employees on ways to turn their goals into habits by identifying where and when they'll complete certain tasks. Social contagion theory? Who cares? Instead, pay attention to the mood you are projecting when you walk into work. If it's not positive, change it.

4. USE THE BACK DOOR

Sometimes in our zeal to introduce a new way of doing things, we throw out all that came before. Sometimes we lose sight of what we're trying to accomplish: to continually improve results. When it comes to influencing your colleagues, your boss, and your company, we offer an alternative that creates much less resistance. We call it the *back door approach*.

The back door approach simply means integrating change into your day-to-day business without any fanfare. You don't need a big announcement. You don't need a PowerPoint presentation. You don't need any capital. You don't even need any permission. What you do need is the courage to try something new. We've removed the risks since all of our tools are backed up by science and have been tested with our clients and other business leaders.

But you don't have to prove anything as you implement these changes. Your results will speak for themselves. As you and your team produce better outcomes, your customer satisfaction scores will go up, your projects will be delivered on time and on budget, and your work environment surveys will begin to outpace those of other departments.

If people become curious, be gracious and share what you've learned. Be open to coaching others on how they too can implement the tools in *Profit from the Positive*. Maybe start a book club

BE A POSITIVE DEVIANT: QUESTIONS THAT LET YOU KNOW YOU'RE ON THE RIGHT TRACK

As you quietly implement the tools in this book, others will become curious. You'll start to hear questions such as the following:

- How did she get those results?

- Why do the people in that department always exceed their plans?

- How is he able to retain top talent when I can't seem to keep anybody?

- Why do her employees seem to really enjoy their work?

- Why does everyone seem so happy to be working over there?

with your peers, team, office, district, or region (see the Reading and Discussion Guide at the end of this book for a summary of each chapter and related discussion questions). Best of all, let these curiosity seekers interview your team and find out firsthand what you and they do to achieve these great results.

Navigating Nuances

Now that you know how to bring the contents of this book to your workplace—by not resisting resistance, starting small, dropping the lingo, and using the back door approach—there are a handful of places in *Profit from the Positive* where two tools may appear to be at odds with each other. Let us clarify: to set or not to set goals, to finish or not to finish, to attract or not to attract differences, to savor or not to savor the past, and to find or not to find solutions.

To set or not to set goals. In Chapter 1, we advised you to "set habits not just goals." Then in Chapter 7 we suggested that you "don't make goals easy and vague" but hard and specific. Which is it? We definitely prefer habits to goals. However, you will likely set a goal on a new endeavor before you will consider converting it into a set of habits. Also, if you lead others, setting challenging and specific goals is necessary to continually improve performance and provide feedback later on.

To finish or not to finish. In Chapter 1, we suggested that you "trick yourself into getting started" by using the Zeigarnik effect: leave something undone in order to remember the activity better when you return to it. However, in the same chapter, we suggested that you "outsource" some of your work to the automatic side of your brain to complete it. Your best choice in some situations may be to complete a task, whereas at other times it may be better to leave some loose ends. Here is one distinction that may help you decide: leaving some loose ends works well when the task requires creative thought. Tasks that are more repetitive in nature are often best left to the automatic side of your brain. You decide.

To attract or not to attract differences. In Chapter 5, we suggested that you "hire for what's not on the resume" by looking for candidates who fit well with your company culture. Remember Zappos.com's weirdness factor and Google's Googliness? However, in Chapter 6, we talked about "turning strengths into a team sport" and discussed well-rounded teams and celebrating differences. So which is it? Embrace what makes your culture quirky and seek out people who will flourish in your environment. However, also be on the lookout for people with skills that can complement your own and your team's.

To savor or not to savor the past. Also in Chapter 5, we advised you to "predict the future by digging into the past." Yet in Chapter 7, we said that you should "preview, don't just review performance." Which is it? Both. It's critically important to dig into a candidate's past to see if she has the right stuff to be successful both in the job and at the company. But once you get employees in the door, get them to imagine the future.

To find or not to find solutions. In Chapter 4, we said to "stop asking the wrong questions" and advised you to focus on what's going right. Later in the chapter we recommended that you "find solutions, not faults." Again, which is it? Both. Finding solutions to problems is important to any business, but you're missing an important factor in the results equation if you don't also mine your company for what's going right.

KEY TAKEAWAYS ─────────

You don't need to be an expert, have a budget, or get your boss's permission to implement the tested tools in *Profit from the Positive*. You can be a positive deviant without anyone ever knowing it. However, don't be surprised when others become curious about the results you are achieving. Remember: you can have more influence both inside and outside your team or business if you do the following:

- **Don't resist resistance.** Expect resistance and you won't be surprised by it. View it as a promising sign of change.

- **Start small.** Don't think you have to wait to use these tools and techniques until your company or HR department changes its policies or practices. Instead, pick three things you can start doing today.

- **Drop the lingo.** A few people may be interested in the field of positive psychology, but don't use jargon with which people are unfamiliar.

- **Use the back door.** Focus on outcomes and let the results speak for themselves.

Curious to learn more? In Appendix F we recommend a number of books, with the selections organized by the chapters in *Profit from the Positive*. We also encourage you to visit our website Profit FromThePositive.com this week for additional resources and to connect with us on Twitter (@profitbook) and Facebook (www.Face book.com/ProfitFromThePositive). Feel free to send us an email at book@ProfitFromThePositive.com with your questions, and of course we always love to hear about what's going right. Let us know which tools you've implemented and what kinds of results you are seeing. What other positive business practices have you and your company implemented? Who knows, maybe we will interview you for our *Profit from the Positive* sequel. Trick yourself into getting started, and you and your company will profit from the positive.

● ● ●   **REFLECTION QUESTIONS** ● ● ●

After reading this chapter, ask yourself these questions:

1. How would I describe this book to a coworker?

2. To whom should I give a copy of this book? Which of my colleagues or friends is a potential positive deviant?

3. Who else is most likely to be supportive of these ideas, and how can I tap into those people?

4. What kind of resistance can I expect from others, and how will I address it?

5. What's one small change I can make right now to profit from the positive?

ALL 31 TOOLS FEATURED IN
PROFIT FROM THE POSITIVE

Objective: Use this summary to assess your current state and track progress.

PART I: IT'S ABOUT THE LEADER

Chapter 1: The Productive Leader: It's More Than Time Management	I will experiment with this tool	I already use this tool	I have mastered this tool
1. Replace "Just Do It" with "Just Plan It"			
2. Trick Yourself into Getting Started			
3. Set Habits, Not Just Goals			
4. Work Less, Accomplish More			

Chapter 2: The Resilient Leader: Give Yourself a Psychological Kick in the Pants	I will experiment with this tool	I already use this tool	I have mastered this tool
1. Don't Quit, Just Quit Being an Expert			
2. Put on an Explorer's Hat			
3. Win Debates Against Yourself			

Chapter 3: The Contagious Leader: Control Your Emotions, Not Your Employees	I will experiment with this tool	I already use this tool	I have mastered this tool
1. Recognize the Achoo! Effect			
2. Tame Your Oscar the Grouch If You Need To			
3. Don't Be a Control Freak			

Chapter 4: The Strengths-Based Leader: Capitalize on What's Right	I will experiment with this tool	I already use this tool	I have mastered this tool
1. Stop Asking the Wrong Questions			
2. Find Solutions, Not Faults			
3. Know Your Strengths or No One Else Will			

PART II: IT'S ABOUT THE TEAM

Chapter 5: Hiring: The Fitness Test	I will experiment with this tool	I already use this tool	I have mastered this tool
1. Hire for What's Not on the Resume			
2. Predict the Future by Digging into the Past			
3. Don't Overlook Your Culture's Quirks			

Chapter 6: Engaging Employees: Bring Out the Best Versus Get the Most	I will experiment with this tool	I already use this tool	I have mastered this tool
1. Don't Just Read the Book			
2. Turn Strengths into a Team Sport			
3. Don't Fire Poor Performers; Fire 'Em Up			
4. Give FRE: Frequent Recognition and Encouragement			

Chapter 7: Performance Reviews: Change 'Em or Chuck 'Em	I will experiment with this tool	I already use this tool	I have mastered this tool
1. Obsess over Strengths but Don't Ignore Weaknesses			
2. Don't Make Goals Easy and Vague			
3. Preview, Don't Just Review, Performance			
4. Chew the Fat; Don't Chew Them Out			

Chapter 8: Meetings: From Energy Buster to Energy Booster	I will experiment with this tool	I already use this tool	I have mastered this tool
1. Start with a Sizzle			
2. Practice the Peak-End Rule			
3. Play Your Whole Bench			

PART III: PUTTING IT ALL TOGETHER

Chapter 9: The Positive Deviant: No Budget? No Problem	I will experiment with this tool	I already use this tool	I have mastered this tool
1. Don't Resist Resistance			
2. Start Small			
3. Drop the Lingo			
4. Use the Back Door			

Is a Strengths-Based Approach a Good Fit for Me?

MANAGER SELF-ASSESSMENT

Objective: Becoming a strengths-based leader is a journey of self-exploration. Complete this quick assessment to find out if a strengths-based approach is a good fit for you.

	Strongly disagree	Disagree	Neither agree nor disagree	Agree	Strongly agree
1. I'm looking for a quick fix to improve results.					
2. Realizing your full potential is more about knowing your weaknesses than about knowing your strengths.					
3. Employees are more productive when they are closely monitored by their manager.					
4. The future of this company is bleak.					
5. I shouldn't have to recognize and encourage people to do a good job; that's what they get paid to do.					
6. I don't have time to develop my people or team.					

	Strongly disagree	Disagree	Neither agree nor disagree	Agree	Strongly agree
7. If employees can't cut it around here, there are plenty of other people out there I can recruit.					
8. I focus on fixing problems and pay little attention to things that are working well.					
9. Getting along with others contributes nothing to achieving results.					
TOTAL					

Scoring Key

- If most of your check marks are in the **first two columns**:

    Bringing a strengths-based approach to your team or business is a great fit. In fact, in many ways you're probably already leading with this approach. In this book you will find additional ways to apply a strengths-based approach.

- If most of your check marks are in the **middle column**:

    Bringing a strengths-based approach to your team or business may be a good fit. Perhaps you are new to managing or so busy that you haven't had the opportunity to explore how you want to lead others. You will find lots of practical tools and techniques in this book to help you.

- If most of your check marks are in the **last two columns**:

   Bringing a strengths-based approach to your team or business is not advised unless you are open to making significant changes in the way you view your role and your employees. You picked up this book or maybe someone passed it along to you, and so you must be curious about what you might learn. Keep reading.

Turn Strengths into a Team Sport

Objective: To guide a discussion with your team to identify, value, and leverage individual and team strengths.

In a roundtable fashion, each team member shares one or more top strengths and talks about the kinds of work that energize and sap energy. Facilitate a discussion with these questions:

1. What do you notice about our team profile? (See the next page for a sample.)

2. Given the nature of our work, how well do our strengths align?

3. Do we have any blind spots? If so, are any important considering the nature of our work? If that is the case, how can we compensate for them?

4. Are there any roles we should tweak or recraft to better align with people's strengths?

5. How can we better capitalize on or leverage one another's strengths? Where should we partner up or collaborate more considering the nature of our strengths and our work?

The Four Leadership Domains*

Team Member	Executing	Influencing	Relationship Building	Strategic Thinking
	Achiever Arranger Belief Consistency Deliberative Discipline Focus Responsibility Restorative	Activator Command Communication Competition Maximizer Self-Assurance Significance Woo	Adaptability Developer Connectedness Empathy Harmony Includer Individualization Positivity Relator	Analytical Context Futuristic Ideation Input Intellection Learner Strategic
Maureen	Deliberative #1 Responsibility #2 Consistency #4 Belief #5		Harmony #3	
Jim	Responsibility #1 Belief #2 Discipline #3 Achiever #5			Strategic #4
Ali	Achiever #2 Responsibility #4 Focus #5			Learner #1 Input #3
Sanjeet	Responsibility #2 Arranger #4 Achiever #5	Maximizer #3	Relator #1	
Joanne	Responsibility #5	Maximizer #4	Harmony #2 Developer #3	Context #1
Bobby		Maximizer #2 Woo #3 Activator #4	Empathy #5	Strategic #1

* Using the language from *StrengthsFinder 2.0* and *Strengths-Based Leadership*.

FREQUENT RECOGNITION AND ENCOURAGEMENT (FRE)

MANAGER SELF-ASSESSMENT

Objective: To determine how much you use recognition and encouragement today to help keep your employees engaged. Place a check in the box that best describes you.

	Strongly disagree	Disagree	Neither agree nor disagree	Agree	Strongly agree
1. I regularly recognize the accomplishments of my employees.					
2. I regularly recognize project milestones.					
3. People often describe me as an enthusiastic supporter of my team.					

	Strongly disagree	Disagree	Neither agree nor disagree	Agree	Strongly agree
4. I recognize even small accomplishments.					
5. I regularly encourage and/ or praise my employees.					
TOTAL					

Scoring Key

- If most of your check marks are in the **first two columns**:

  You have a huge opportunity to reap the productivity gains associated with giving frequent recognition and encouragement.

- If most of your check marks are in the **middle column**:

  You are probably doing a number of things right. Be even more intentional about giving FRE. You will find a number of practical tools and techniques in this book to help you.

- If most of your check marks are in the **last two columns**:

  You and your employees are already reaping the benefits associated with FRE and are great role models for others. Keep doing what you're doing.

EMPLOYEE ASSESSMENT OF MANAGER

Objective: To provide your manager with feedback on how well he or she provides recognition and encouragement to you and other employees. Place a check in the box that best describes your perspective.

	Strongly disagree	Disagree	Neither agree nor disagree	Agree	Strongly agree
1. My manager recognizes my accomplishments regularly.					
2. My manager regularly recognizes project milestones.					
3. I would describe my manager as an enthusiastic supporter of our team.					
4. My manager notices even small accomplishments.					
5. My manager regularly encourages and/ or praises me.					
TOTAL					

Please return this assessment to your manager.

Scoring Key

- If most of your employees' check marks are in **the first two columns**:

  You have a huge opportunity to reap the productivity gains associated with giving frequent recognition and encouragement.

- If most of your employees' check marks are in the **middle column**:

  You may want to follow up with your employees individually and find out what they are thinking. Could they be afraid to provide candid answers?

- If most of your employees' check marks are in the **last two columns**:

  Your employees feel valued and appreciated and are more likely to be highly engaged and productive.

Compare Your Self-Assessment with Your Employees' Assessments

- How closely did your self-assessment match your employees' views of you?

- What are one or two actions you can do to make recognition more of a habit?

The Five FRESH Themes

In *Profit from the Positive*, five big themes emerge. We call them FRESH: **F**it, **R**ight, **E**motions, **S**cience, and **H**abits. This might be an easy shorthand way to introduce the concepts in this book to others.

Fit: What's fit? Fit shows up in our hiring practices—both job fit and company fit. Fit also shows up in the way we align work to an employee's strengths. When it comes to recruiting new employees, we need to expand our view of what good fit really means. Today we tend to focus on the candidate's technical skills, education, and experience. We discount the importance of interpersonal skills and how well the candidate will fit in at our company. Once employees are hired, we spend too much time shining a spotlight on their weaknesses rather than their strengths. You're probably familiar with the old adage, "He's a square peg in a round hole." That's what happens when we don't pay attention to fit. Instead, we need to talk to employees (and not just once or twice a year) about how they can create a better fit between their strengths and their jobs.

Right: What's right? Most of us have been educated and trained to look for what's wrong. It's often the lens through which we view the world. We solve problems. We close gaps. We fix people and things. Operating your business from this deficit approach is going to get you only so far. We're skilled in conducting postmortems so that we can prevent the same mistakes from reoccurring in the future. Rarely, however, do we apply the same diagnostic rigor to analyzing what went right. Imagine replicating what's going right in one area of your business to another area. How might that improve your results? The deficit approach is often applied to managing people, too. If all you do is look at what your employees do wrong or focus only on fixing their weaknesses, you are missing out on two significant motivators: strengths and recognition.

Emotions: What are you transmitting? Our emotions, both positive and negative, are highly contagious. Positive emotions expand our creativity, whereas negative emotions shut it down. The way you conduct yourself from the moment you walk into the office or workplace matters. The way you conduct meetings matter too. Why? Because your emotions can have a positive or a negative impact not only on your own productivity, but also on your employees' productivity.

Science: What's the scientific evidence? *Profit from the Positive* is not a self-help book espousing someone's opinion. Instead, we've shared over 30 tools that are backed by science and are being used by successful business leaders today.

Habits: What can you turn into a habit? We tend to waste a lot of time thinking about what we *will* do. Many of us are chronic contemplators—"I will write that report," "I will call that customer," "I will work out"—rather than determined doers. The more tasks we can outsource to the automatic side of our brains, the more productive we will be and the more time we will have to focus our conscious thought on what's most important to us. Most of the tools in *Profit from the Positive* can easily be turned into a habit, such as starting your meetings on a positive note, devoting 10 minutes to planning your day, and giving frequent recognition and encouragement.

GOOD READS

Curious to learn more? Here are some books we recommend, organized by chapter.

CHAPTER 1: THE PRODUCTIVE LEADER: IT'S MORE THAN TIME MANAGEMENT

1. Replace "Just Do It" with "Just Plan It"

The Checklist Manifesto: How to Get Things Right by Atul Gawande
Changing for Good: A Revolutionary Six-Stage Program for Overcoming Bad Habits and Moving Your Life Positively Forward by James O. Prochaska, John C. Norcross, and Carlo C. DiClemente

2. Trick Yourself into Getting Started

One Small Step Can Change Your Life: The Kaizen Way by Robert Maurer
Getting Things Done: The Art of Stress-Free Productivity by David Allen

3. Set Habits, Not Just Goals

The Power of Habit: Why We Do What We Do in Life and Business by
Charles Duhigg

4. Work Less, Accomplish More

*Sleeping with Your Smartphone: How to Break the 24/7 Habit and
Change the Way You Work* by Leslie Perlow

*Smarts and Stamina: The Busy Person's Guide to Optimal Health
and Performance* by Marie-Josée Shaar and Kathryn Britton

CHAPTER 2: THE RESILIENT LEADER:
GIVE YOURSELF A PSYCHOLOGICAL
KICK IN THE PANTS

1. Don't Quit, Just Quit Being an Expert

Why Zebras Don't Get Ulcers by Robert M. Sapolsky

Mindset: The New Psychology of Success by Carol S. Dweck

Curious? Discover the Missing Ingredient to a Fulfilling Life by Todd
Kashdan

2. Put on an Explorer's Hat

Learned Optimism: How to Change Your Mind and Your Life by Martin
E. P. Seligman

*The Resilience Factor: 7 Essentials Skills for Overcoming Life's Inevitable
Obstacles* by Karen Reivich and Andrew Shatté

Resilience: How to Navigate Life's Curves, edited by Senia Maymin
and Kathryn Britton

3. Win Debates Against Yourself

Peak: How Great Companies Get Their Mojo from Maslow by Chip
Conley

Taming Your Gremlin: A Surprisingly Simple Method for Getting Out of Your Own Way by Rick Carson

CHAPTER 3: THE CONTAGIOUS LEADER: CONTROL YOUR EMOTIONS, NOT YOUR EMPLOYEES

1. Recognize the Achool Effect

Positivity: Top Notch Research Reveals the 3 to 1 Ratio That Will Change Your Life by Barbara Fredrickson

2. Tame Your Oscar the Grouch If You Need To

The Law of the Garbage Truck: How to Respond to People Who Dump on You, and How to Stop Dumping on Others by David J. Pollay

3. Don't Be a Control Freak

The No-Asshole Rule: Building a Civilized Workplace and Surviving One That Isn't by Robert I. Sutton

CHAPTER 4: THE STRENGTHS-BASED LEADER: CAPITALIZE ON WHAT'S RIGHT

1. Stop Asking the Wrong Questions

What Got You Here Won't Get You There: How Successful People Become Even More Successful by Marshall Goldsmith

2. Find Solutions, Not Faults

Give and Take: A Revolutionary Approach to Success by Adam M. Grant

3. Know Your Strengths or No One Else Will

Strengths Based Leadership: Great Leaders, Teams, and Why People Follow by Tom Rath and Barry Conchie

CHAPTER 5: HIRING:
THE FITNESS TEST

1. Hire for What's Not on the Resume

101 Smart Questions to Ask on Your Interview by Ron Fry
101 Great Answers to the Toughest Interview Questions by Ron Fry

2. Predict the Future by Digging into the Past

Thinking, Fast and Slow by Daniel Kahneman

3. Don't Overlook Your Culture's Quirks

Delivering Happiness: A Path to Profits, Passion, and Purpose by
Tony Hsieh

CHAPTER 6: ENGAGING EMPLOYEES:
BRING OUT THE BEST VERSUS GET THE MOST

1. Don't Just Read the Book

Ha! We are not recommending a book here.

2. Turn Strengths into a Team Sport

*Strengths Based Leadership: Great Leaders, Teams, and Why People
Follow* by Tom Rath and Barry Conchie
Go Put Your Strengths to Work by Marcus Buckingham

3. Don't Fire Poor Performers; Fire 'Em Up

Flow: The Psychology of Optimal Experience by Mihaly Csikszentmihalyi
*High Impact Leader: Moments Matter in Accelerating Authentic Lead-
ership Development* by Bruce J. Avolio and Fred Luthans

4. Give FRE: Frequent Recognition and Encouragement

Encouraging the Heart: A Leader's Guide to Rewarding and Recognizing Others by James Kouzes and Barry Posner

Energize Your Workplace: How to Create and Sustain High-Quality Connections at Work by Jane E. Dutton

How Full Is Your Bucket? Positive Strategies for Work and Life by Tom Rath

CHAPTER 7: PERFORMANCE REVIEWS: CHANGE 'EM OR CHUCK 'EM

1. Obsess over Strengths But Don't Ignore Weaknesses

Drive: The Surprising Truth About What Motivates Us by Dan H. Pink

2. Don't Make Goals Easy and Vague

Succeed: How We Can Reach Our Goals by Heidi Grant Halvorson and Carol S. Dweck

3. Preview, Don't Just Review, Performance

The Power of Full Engagement: Managing Energy, Not Time, Is the Key to High Performance and Personal Renewal by Jim Loehr and Tony Schwartz

Making Hope Happen: Create the Future You Want for Yourself and Others by Shane Lopez

4. Chew the Fat; Don't Chew Them Out

Crucial Conversations: Tools for Talking When Stakes Are High, second edition, by Kerry Patterson, Joseph Grenny, Ron McMillan, and Al Switzler

Difficult Conversations: How to Discuss What Matters Most by Douglas Stone, Bruce Patton, Sheila Heen, and Roger Fisher

CHAPTER 8: MEETINGS:
FROM ENERGY BUSTER TO ENERGY BOOSTER

The Thin Book of Appreciative Inquiry by Sue Annis Hammond
The Appreciative Inquiry Summit: A Practitioner's Guide for Leading Large-Group Change by James D. Ludema, Diane Whitney, Bernard J. Mohr, and Thomas J. Griffin

CHAPTER 9—THE POSITIVE DEVIANT:
NO BUDGET? NO PROBLEM

Good Reads About Leading Change

Made to Stick: Why Some Ideas Survive and Others Die by Chip Heath and Dan Heath
Switch: How to Change Things When Things are Hard by Chip Heath and Dan Heath
Building the Bridge as You Walk on It: A Guide to Leading Change by Robert E. Quinn
Positive Organizational Scholarship: Foundations of a New Discipline, edited by Kim S. Cameron, Jane E. Dutton, and Robert E. Quinn

Good Reads About Positive Psychology

Authentic Happiness: Using the New Positive Psychology to Realize Your Full Potential for Lasting Fulfillment by Martin E. P. Seligman

Flourish: A Visionary New Understanding of Happiness and Well-Being by Martin E. P. Seligman

Happier: Learn the Secrets of Daily Joy and Lasting Fulfillment by Tal Ben-Shahar

The Happiness Advantage: The Seven Principles That Fuel Success and Performance at Work by Shawn Achor

The Happiness Hypothesis: Finding Modern Truth in Ancient Wisdom by Jonathan Haidt

The How of Happiness: A New Approach to Getting the Life You Want by Sonja Lyubomirsky

A Primer in Positive Psychology by Christopher Peterson

Scan PositivePsychologyNews.com, a site Senia founded in 2006 that has over 1,000 articles on positive psychology research by over 100 authors.

References

INTRODUCTION: YOU'VE TRIED EVERYTHING. NOW TRY SOMETHING THAT WORKS

For an introduction to the broad scope of research in positive psychology, refer to over 1,000 research-based articles by over 100 authors at Positive-PsychologyNews.com.

The original academic article on positive psychology: Seligman, M. E. P., and Csikszentmihalyi, M. (2000). Positive psychology: An introduction. *American Psychologist, 55,* 5–14.

"... over 10,000 research papers have been written." Based on Rusk, R. D., and Waters, L. E. (2013). Tracing the size, reach, impact, and breadth of positive psychology. *The Journal of Positive Psychology, 8*(3), 207–221. We gratefully acknowledge additional data received directly from Reuben D. Rusk and Lea. E. Waters.

CHAPTER 1: THE PRODUCTIVE LEADER: IT'S MORE THAN TIME MANAGEMENT

Introduction

"Seventy percent of Americans report ..." American Psychological Association. (2010). Stress in America, 2010. Retrieved from http://www.apa .org/news/press/releases/stress/national-report.pdf.

"Americans on average work eight hours more per week ..." Stansberry, G. (2010). Why Germans have longer vacation time and more productivity. *OPEN Forum.* Retrieved from http://www.openforum.com/idea-hub /topics/lifestyle/article/why-germans-have-longer-vacation-times-and -more-productivity-glen-stansberry.

"Sociologists have been asking people to keep time diaries ..." Robinson, J. P., & Godbey, G. (1999). *Time for life: The surprising ways Americans use their time.* Pennsylvania: Pennsylvania University Press. Cited in Stromberg, P. G. (2011). I'm so busy. *Psychology Today* blog. Retrieved from http:// www.psychologytoday.com/blog/sex-drugs-and-boredom/201101 /im-so-busy.

"Marissa Mayer stated previously, 'I do marathon email catch-up sessions ...'" Mayer, M. (2006). How I work. *Fortune*. Retrieved from http://money .cnn.com/popups/2006/fortune/how_i_work/frameset.exclude.html.

"Mayer describes regularly working 90-hour weeks ..." Lublin, J. S. (2012). Making sure "busy" doesn't lead to burnout. *Wall Street Journal online*. Retrieved from http://online.wsj.com/article/SB1000142405270230382220457746465376432534.html.

"... we lose up to 40 percent of our productivity from flip-flopping ..." American Psychological Association. (2006). *Multi-tasking: Switching costs*. Retrieved from http://www.apa.org/research/action/multitask .aspx.

"... $650 billion annually..." Lohr, S. (2007). Is information overload a $650 billion drag on the economy? *New York Times*. Retrieved from http://bits .blogs.nytimes.com/2007/12/20/is-information-overload-a-650-billion -drag-on-the-economy/.

"... $70 billion a year ..." Day, M. (2008). Hi-tech is turning us all into time-wasters. *The Observer*. Retrieved from http://www.guardian.co.uk /science/2008/jul/20/psychology.mobilephones.

"... Jeff Taylor, founder and formerly Chief Monster of Monster.com ..." Petrecca, L. (2011). Jeff Taylor: Founder of Monster.com. *USA Today*. Retrieved from http://usatoday30.usatoday.com/MONEY/usaedition /2011-04-11-Small-Business-Challenge_ST2_U.htm.

"Researchers have found that perfectionism results ..." Chin, E. (2009). Perfectionism and productivity: Visions of success or fear of failure? *Positive Psychology News Daily*. Retrieved from http://positivepsychologynews .com/news/eleanor-chin/200909154085.

1. Replace "Just Do It" with "Just Plan It"

"Psychologist Peter Gollwitzer ... recruited university students ..." Gollwitzer, P. M. (1993). Goal achievement: The role of intentions. *European Review of Social Psychology 4(1)*, 141–185.

"Gollwitzer's study has been replicated about 100 times ..." Gollwitzer, P. M., & Sheeran, P. (2006). Implementation intentions and goal achievement: A meta-analysis of effects and processes. *Advances in Experimental Social Psychology, 38*, 69–119.

"Psychologist James Prochaska developed a model for the ways people create change in their lives ..." Prochaska, J. O., Norcross, J. C., & DiClemente, C. C. (1994). *Changing for Good*. New York: Morrow.

2. Trick Yourself into Getting Started

"The Zeigarnik Effect" Zeigarnik, B. (1927). Das Behalten erledigter und un-
    erledigter Handlungen (On finished and unfinished tasks). *Psychologische
    Forschung, 9*, 1–85.

"... Wash Your Car for the First Time or the Third Time?" Nunez, J. C., &
    Dreze, X. (2006). The endowed progress effect: How artificial advance-
    ment increases effort. *Journal of Consumer Research, 32*, 504–512.

"One Minute in Front of the TV," Maurer, R. (2004). *One small step can change
    your life: The kaizen way.* New York: Workman Publishing Company.
    Macfarlane, D. J., Taylor, L. H. & Cuddihy, T. F. (2006). Very short inter-
    mittent versus continuous bouts of activity in sedentary adults. *Preven-
    tive Medicine*, 43(4), 332–336.

3. Set Habits, Not Just Goals

"What We Can Learn from Drug Addicts." Smith, K. S., Virkud, A., De-
    isseroth, K, & Graybiel, A. M. (2012). Reversible online control of ha-
    bitual behavior by optogenetic perturbation of medial prefrontal cortex.
    Proceedings of the National Academy of Sciences,109(46), 18932–7; Barnes,
    T. D., Kubota Y., Hu, D, Jin, D. Z., & Graybiel, A. M. (2005). Activity
    of striatal neurons reflects dynamic encoding and recoding of procedural
    memories. *Nature, 437*, 1158–1161.

"Psychologist Wendy Wood ... the ability of students to stick with a positive
    habit ..." Wood, W., Tam, L., & Guerrero Witt, M. (2005). Changing
    circumstances, disrupting habits. *Journal of Personality and Social Psychol-
    ogy, 88*, 918–933.

4. Work Less, Accomplish More

"Cases of insomnia, alcoholism, and caffeine addiction are increasing, and
    all can be linked to an increasingly stressful lifestyle." Sinha, R. (2008).
    Chronic stress, drug use, and vulnerability to addiction. *Annals of the New
    York Academy of Sciences, 1141(1)*, 105–130.

"Author of *Sleeping with your Smartphone* and Harvard Business School pro-
    fessor Leslie Perlow ..." Perlow, L. A. (2012). *Sleeping with your smart-
    phone: How to break the 24/7 habit and change the way you work.* Harvard
    Business Press.

"Sony Pictures Entertainment has figured out ..." Schwartz, T. (2010). The
    productivity paradox: How Sony Pictures gets more out of people by
    demanding less. *Harvard Business Review*. Retrieved from http://hbr

.org/2010/06/the-productivity-paradox-how-sony-pictures-gets-more
-out-of-people-by-demanding-less/ar/1.

"... mainstream corporations such as General Mills, Target, and Aetna ..."
Gelles, D. (2012). The mind business. *FT Magazine*. Retrieved from
http://www.ft.com/intl/cms/s/2/d9cb7940-ebea-11e1–985a-0014
4feab49a.html.

"Aetna's chairman and CEO Mark Bertolini ..." Gelles (2012).

"They all invested in EverFi ..." *Washington Business Journal* (2012). EverFi
raises $10M from Jeff Bezos, Eric Schmidt. Retrieved from http://www
.bizjournals.com/washington/news/2012/08/15/everfi-raises-10m-from
-jeff-bezos.html; Davidson, T. Personal interview. December 17, 2012.

CHAPTER 2: THE RESILIENT LEADER: GIVE YOURSELF A PSYCHOLOGICAL KICK IN THE PANTS

Introduction

"'If you want to be inventive, you have to be willing to fail,' says ... Jeff
Bezos." Anders, G. (2012). Jeff Bezos reveals his no. 1 leadership secret.
Forbes. Retrieved from http://www.forbes.com/forbes/2012/0423/ceo
-compensation-12-amazon-technology-jeff-bezos-gets-it_7.html.

"A 2012 global study of over 16,000 employees...." The Regus Group. 2012.
From distressed to de-stressed. Retrieved from http://www.regus.com
/stress-report.

"PTSD or Post-Traumatic Growth?" Britton, K. H. (2011). Putting the
world back together differently. *Positive Psychology News Daily*. Retrieved from http://positivepsychologynews.com/news/kathryn
-britton/2011053017972; Johnson, L. L. C. (2009). Beyond resilience:
Growth after adversity. *Positive Psychology News Daily*. Retrieved
from http://positivepsychologynews.com/news/laura-lc-johnson
/200905251927.

"If anyone knows about traumatic events, it's the first responders who show
up on the scene...." Shakespeare-Finch, J. E., Smith, S. G., Gow, K. M.,
Embelton, G., & Baird, L. (2003). The prevalence of post-traumatic
growth in emergency ambulance personnel. *Traumatology, 9(1)*, 58–71.

1. Don't Quit, Just Quit Being an Expert

"Chip Conley is the founder of Joie de Vivre Hotels." Conley, C. (2007). *Peak:
How great companies get their mojo from Maslow*. New York: Jossey-Bass;
Conley, C. Personal interview. December 27, 2012.

"For decades, Stanford psychologist Carol Dweck has been studying . . ." Elliott, E. S., & Dweck, C. S. (1988). Goals: An approach to motivation and achievement. *Journal of Personality and Social Psychology, 54(1)*, 5–12. To read more about learning and performance goals and organizations: Murphy, M. C., & Dweck, C. S. (2010). A culture of genius: How an organization's lay theory shapes people's cognition, affect, and behavior. *Personality and Social Psychology Bulletin, 36(3)*, 283–296.

"Mistake-of-the-Month Club." Conley, C. Personal interview. December 27, 2012.

"Bezos believes that a desire to invent and explore—what we call a learning mindset—is necessary at all levels of the company. . . ." Hof, R. (2012). Jeff Bezos: How Amazon web services is just like the Kindle business. *Forbes*. Retrieved from http://www.forbes.com/sites/roberthof/2012/11/29 /jeff-bezos-how-amazon-web-services-is-just-like-the-kindle-business/.

2. Put on an Explorer's Hat

"Our mentor Martin Seligman is the author of *Learned Optimism* . . ." Seligman, M. E. (1991). *Learned optimism: How to change your mind and your life*. New York: Knopf.

"The Me-Always-Everything Framework" Reivich, K., & Shatté, A. (2003). *The resilience factor: 7 keys to finding your inner strength and overcoming life's hurdles*. New York: Broadway Books.

"Nido Qubein knows a thing or two about being resilient . . ." Qubein, N. Personal interview. May 12, 2009.

3. Win Debates Against Yourself

"CBT is a highly effective tool for eliminating psychological issues, including panic attacks." Seligman, M. E. (1993). *What you can change and what you can't: The complete guide to successful self-improvement*. New York: Knopf.

CHAPTER 3: THE CONTAGIOUS LEADER: CONTROL YOUR EMOTIONS, NOT YOUR EMPLOYEES

Introduction

"In a study of 358 managers at Johnson & Johnson . . ." Cavallo, K., & Brienza, D. (2006). Emotional competence and leadership excellence at Johnson & Johnson. *Europe's Journal of Psychology, 2(1)*. Retrieved from http://

ejop.psychopen.eu/article/view/313/221 and http://www.the-isei.com/Libraries/Articles/Johnson_Johnson_EI_Study.sflb.ashx.

1. Recognize the Achoo! Effect

"Sigal Barsade . . . claims that we can unconsciously catch both good and bad moods . . ." Barsade, S. G. (2002). The ripple effect: Emotional contagion and its influence on group behavior. *Administrative Science Quarterly, 47(4)*, 644–675.

"In another study, researchers observed over 200 customer service interactions at a coffee shop." As cited in this review paper: Barsade, S. G., & Gibson, D. E. (2007). Why does affect matter in organizations? *Academy of Management Perspectives, 21(1)*, 36–59.

"Researchers have also found that a leader's positive or negative mood can spread in as little as seven minutes." Sy, T., Côté, S., & Saavedra, R. (2005). The contagious leader: Impact of the leader's mood on the mood of group members, group affective tone, and group processes. *Journal of Applied Psychology, 90(2)*, 295.

"In a study of 53 sales managers . . ." George, J. M. (2006). Leader positive mood and group performance: The case of customer service. *Journal of Applied Social Psychology, 25(9)*, 778–794.

"Cindi Bigelow, president of Bigelow Tea, sums it up this way: . . ." Bigelow, C. Speech at the Women's Congress in 2007, Boston, MA.

"Bigelow acknowledges that leaders must get results and move the company forward . . ." Nextforwomen (2012). Cindi Bigelow of Bigelow Tea on being sincere to your core. Retrieved from http://www.youtube.com/watch?v=jJzCG_fsmQw.

"Jason Fried, CEO of 37signals . . ." 37signals (2006). *Getting real.* Retrieved from http://gettingreal.37signals.com/3705222012-getting_real.pdf.

2. Tame Your Oscar the Grouch If You Need To

"One of the most famous and earliest studies of embodiment is the pen smile study." Strack, F., Martin, L. L., & Stepper, S. (1988). Inhibiting and facilitating conditions of the human smile: A nonobtrusive test of the facial feedback hypothesis. *Journal of Personality and Social Psychology, 54(5)*, 768.

3. Don't Be a Control Freak

"Psychologists can code such beliefs by their *locus of control*." There is a lot of research in this area. For example: Spector, P. E. (2011). Development of the work locus of control scale. *Journal of Occupational Psychology, 61(4)*, 335–340; Spectora, P. E. (1982). Behavior in organizations as a function of employee's locus of control. *Psychological Bulletin, 91(3)*, 482–497.

CHAPTER 4: THE STRENGTHS-BASED LEADER: CAPITALIZE ON WHAT'S RIGHT

Introduction

"In their journal article 'Bad is Stronger than Good' . . ." Baumeister, R. F., Bratslavsky, E., Finkenauer, C., & Vohs, K. D. (2001). Bad is stronger than good. *Review of General Psychology, 5(4)*, 323–370.

1. Stop Asking the Wrong Questions

"Research by New York University psychology professor Tory Higgins and his colleagues . . ." Higgins, E. T. (1998). Promotion and prevention: Regulatory focus as a motivational principle. *Advances in Experimental Social Psychology, 30*, 1–46.

"That's what NUMMI (New United Motor Manufacturing, Inc.), a joint venture between Toyota and GM, did to improve processes." Former NUMMI employee. Personal communication. March 3, 2011.

". . . facilitate a SOAR analysis instead: *s*trengths, *o*pportunities, *a*spirations, and *r*esults." Horne, A. (2010). SOAR—Workshop review. *Positive Psychology News Daily*. Retrieved from http://positivepsychologynews.com/news/amanda-horne/2010090313242; Stavros, J. (2009). *The thin book of SOAR: Building strengths-based strategy*. Bend, OR: Thin Book Publishing.

2. Find Solutions, Not Faults

"In a research study Margaret conducted with our University of Pennsylvania classmate Dana Arakawa . . ." Arakawa, D., & Greenberg, M. (2007). Optimistic managers and their influence on productivity and employee engagement in a technology organization: Implications for coaching psychologists. *International Coaching Psychology Review, 2*, 78–89.

3. Know Your Strengths or No One Else Will

"For example, Gallup conducted a study with Marriott Vacation Club salespeople." Rath, T. (2011). Strength makes sales increase. Retrieved from http://www.youtube.com/watch?v=WLL2xy5eQTQ.

"Gallup interviewed nearly 200,000 employees in 36 companies . . ." Harter, J. Taking feedback to the bottom line. *Gallup Business Journal.* Retrieved from http://businessjournal.gallup.com/content/814/taking-feedback -bottom-line.aspx; Buckingham, M., & Clifton, D. O. The strengths revolution. *Gallup Business Journal.* Retrieved from http://businessjournal.gal lup.com/content/547/the-strengths-revolution.aspx; Gallup. *Employee engagement: A leading indicator of financial performance.* Retrieved from http://www.gallup.com/consulting/52/employee-engagement.aspx.

"As Steve Jobs, former Apple CEO, said in his commencement speech at Stanford . . ." Jobs, S. (2005). "For the past 33 years, I have looked in the mirror every morning . . ." Jobs says. *Stanford Report.* Retrieved from http://news.stanford.edu/news/2005/june15/jobs-061505.html.

"Martin Seligman clarifies, 'Working hard to manage weaknesses . . .'" Seligman, M. (2005). Class discussion. Master of Applied Positive Psychology.

CHAPTER 5: HIRING: THE FITNESS TEST

Introduction

"Studies by a human resources consulting company found that every hire costs a company up to five times . . ." Yager, F. (2012). The cost of bad hiring decisions runs high. *Dice.* Retrieved from http://resources.dice.com /report/the-cost-of-bad-hiring-decisions/.

"Zappos.com CEO Tony Hsieh says, 'If you add up all the bad decisions of the bad hires made . . ." Fass, A. (2012). Tony Hsieh: ". . . in the course of Zappos's history, it's probably cost us over $100 million." *Inc.com.* Retrieved from http://www.inc.com/allison-fass/tony-hsieh-hiring-mistakes-cost -zappos-100-million.html.

"In Senia's research with her colleagues at Stanford, she found that people are drawn to the familiar . . ." Litt, A., Reich, T., Maymin, S., & Shiv, B. (2011). Pressure and perverse flights to familiarity. *Psychological Science, 22(4),* 523–531.

"One of the main qualities most employers want is the candidate's ability to work well with others." Zupek, R. (2011). Top 10 reasons employers want to hire you. CareerBuilder.com. Retrieved from http://www.cnn .com/2009/LIVING/worklife/11/02/cb.hire.reasons.job/index.html.

1. Hire for What's Not on the Resume

"Martin Seligman struck up a conversation with the man sitting next to him . . ." Seligman, M. E. (1991). *Learned optimism: How to change your mind and your life.* New York: Knopf.

"In a review of job descriptions at over 100 Fortune 500 companies, emotional intelligence author and psychologist Daniel Goleman ..." Goleman, D. (2006). *Emotional intelligence: Why it can matter more than IQ.* New York: Bantam.

"Taking initiative, for example, has been shown to correlate with productivity according to researcher Michael Frese ..." Frese, M., Fay, D., Hilburger, T., Leng, K., & Tag, A. (2011). The concept of personal initiative: Operationalization, reliability and validity in two German samples. *Journal of Occupational and Organizational Psychology, 70(2),* 139–161.

"Microsoft CEO Steve Ballmer said, 'I try to figure out sort of a combination of IQ and passion.'" Bryant, A. (2009). Meetings, version 2.0, at Microsoft. *New York Times:* "Corner Office." Retrieved from http://www.nytimes.com/2009/05/17/business/17corner.html?.

2. Predict the Future by Digging into the Past

"Professor Amy Wrzesniewski at the Yale School of Management has studied various professions ..." Wrzesniewski, A., McCauley, C., Rozin, P., & Schwartz, B. (1997). Jobs, careers, and callings: People's relations to their work. *Journal of Research in Personality, 31(1),* 21–33; Wrzesniewski, A., & Dutton, J. E. (2001). Crafting a job: Revisioning employees as active crafters of their work. *Academy of Management Review, 26(2),* 179–201.

3. Don't Overlook Your Culture's Quirks

"Googly." Gordon, C. (2012). Google is hiring: The secret to getting a job at Google, AOL jobs. Retrieved from http://jobs.aol.com/articles/2012/08/24/want-to-get-a-job-at-google-heres-how/.

"Hsieh explains: 'Today, when we interview, we have questions for each one of the core values.'" Bryant, A. (2010). On a scale of 1 to 10, how weird are you? *New York Times:* "Corner Office." Retrieved from http://www.nytimes.com/2010/01/10/business/10corner.html?.

"Christa Foley, senior manager of HR at Zappos University, told us...." Foley, C. Personal email interview, responses on December 13, 2012.

"Passion in the Workplace" Peterson, C., Park, N., Hall, N., & Seligman, M. E. (2009). Zest and work. *Journal of Organizational Behavior, 30(2),* 161–172.

"Rackspace, a 2,000-employee web hosting company known for its impeccable customer service, says, 'We'd rather miss a good one than hire a bad one.'" Simon, E. (2007). Employers study applicants' personalities. *Washington*

Post. Retrieved from http://www.washingtonpost.com/wp-dyn/content /article/2007/11/05/AR2007110500960_pf.html.

CHAPTER 6: ENGAGING EMPLOYEES: BRING OUT THE BEST VERSUS GET THE MOST

Introduction

"But the satisfaction measure left out an important factor: the link between enjoying one's job and the company's profitability." Overview paper that describes measuring emotion and happiness as opposed to satisfaction on pages 42–43; Barsade, S. G., & Gibson, D. E. (2007). Why does affect matter in organizations? *Academy of Management Perspectives, 21(1)*, 36–59.

"Today, successful companies such as Best Buy and Ann Taylor, among others, are focusing instead on *employee engagement. . ."* Chong, W. How Ann Taylor invests in talent. *Gallup Business Journal.* Retrieved from http:// businessjournal.gallup.com/content/25351/how-ann-taylor-invests -talent.aspx; Strengths @ BestBuy. Retrieved from http://bestbuystrengths .com/Know_Your_Strengths.html.

". . . Gallup has found that employees who have the opportunity to focus on their strengths every day are six times more likely to be engaged in their jobs." Asplunt, J. (2012). Seven reasons to lead with strengths, *Gallup Blog.* Retrieved from http://thegallupblog.gallup.com/2012/09 /seven-reasons-to-lead-with-strengths.html; Asplunt, J., & Blacksmith, N. (2012). Embedding strengths in your company's DNA. *Gallup Business Journal.* Retrieved from http://businessjournal.gallup.com /content/155036/embedding-strengths-company-dna.aspx.

"Unfortunately, according to the latest Gallup global statistics, only 30 percent of employees worldwide are engaged in their jobs." Blacksmith, N. & Harter, J. (2011). Majority of American workers not engaged in their jobs. *Gallup Wellbeing.* Retrieved from http://www.gallup.com /poll/150383/majority-american-workers-not-engaged-jobs.aspx.

1. Don't Just Read the Book

"Studies of more than 300,000 employees in 51 companies showed . . ." Harter, J. K., & Schmidt, F. L. (2002). *Employee engagement, satisfaction, and business-unit-level outcomes: Meta-analysis.* Princeton, NJ: Gallup Organization.

"Specifically, projects that were led by managers who scored in the top quartile for focusing on their employees' strengths achieved better results." Arakawa, D., & Greenberg, M. (2007). Optimistic managers and their influence on productivity and employee engagement in a technology organization: Implications for coaching psychologists. *International Coaching Psychology Review, 2*, 78–89.

"Our University of Pennsylvania classmate Gordon Parry, president of the Aristotle Group, ran a job-crafting study." Parry, G. H. (2006). Recrafting work: A model for workplace engagement and meaning. *University of Pennsylvania Scholarly Commons.*

2. Turn Strengths into a Team Sport

"'From earlier research we know great leaders never need to be well rounded, but great teams probably do,' says Tom Rath ..." Rath, T. Personal interview. February 2009.

3. Don't Fire Poor Performers; Fire 'Em Up

"Csikszentmihalyi called that feeling flow." Csikszentmihalyi, M. (1990). *Flow: The psychology of optimal experience.* New York: Harper & Row.

4. Give FRE: Frequent Recognition and Encouragement

"Imagine that you could improve productivity by over 40 percent." Arakawa, D., & Greenberg, M. (2007). Optimistic managers and their influence on productivity and employee engagement in a technology organization: Implications for coaching psychologists. *International Coaching Psychology Review, 2*, 78–89.

"Research studies by Carol Dweck of Stanford University have found that process praise is more effective than person praise." Kamins, M. L., & Dweck, C. S. (1999). Person versus process praise and criticism: Implications for contingent self-worth and coping. *Developmental Psychology, 35(3)*, 835.

"... says Robert A. Eckert, who retired in 2012 as chairman of the world's largest toy company, Mattel." Eckert, R. A. (2013). The two most important words. *Harvard Business Review.* Retrieved from http://hbr.org/2013/04/the-two-most-important-words.

"Christa Foley, senior manager of HR at Zappos University, told us...." Foley, C. Personal email interview, responses on December 13, 2012.

"'Stab in the heart and praise to the back,' says EverFi's Tom Davidson." Davidson, T. Personal interview. December 17, 2012.

"...David C. Novak, chairman, CEO, and president of Yum! Brands..." Bryant, A. (2009). At Yum! Brands, rewards for good work. *New York Times*: "Corner Office." Retrieved from http://www.nytimes.com/2009/07/12 /business/12corner.html?pagewanted=all.

CHAPTER 7: PERFORMANCE REVIEWS: CHANGE 'EM OR CHUCK 'EM

Introduction

"...we artificially rank people..." Dvorak. J. C. (2012). Attacking stack ranking. *PCMag.com*. Retrieved from http://www.pcmag.com/article2 /0,2817,2406673,00.asp; Cohan. P. (2012). Why stack ranking worked better at GE than Microsoft. *Forbes*. Retrieved from http://www.forbes .com/sites/petercohan/2012/07/13/why-stack-ranking-worked-better -at-ge-than-microsoft/.

"In a 2012 study by the Society of Human Resource Management, 45 percent of HR leaders ..." SHRM/Globoforce (2012). Employee recognition survey: Winter 2012 report. SHRM/Globoforce. Retrieved from http://go.globoforce.com/SHRM-winter-2012-report_announcement .html and http://go.globoforce.com/rs/globoforce/images/SHRM Winter2012Report.PDF.

"Performance reviews 'mostly suck,' says Robert Sutton, a Stanford University management professor." McGregor, J. (2009). Performance review takes a page from Facebook. *Bloomberg Businessweek*. Retrieved from http:// www.businessweek.com/stories/2009–03–11/performance-review -takes-a-page-from-facebook.

1. Obsess over Strengths but Don't Ignore Weaknesses

"In a Corporate Leadership Council's study of over 20,000 employees in 29 countries, researchers found that focusing on employee strengths during reviews led to a 36 percent improvement in performance." SHRM HR News (2008). *The Power of Positive Thinking in the Workplace*. Retrieved from http://www.shrm.org/Publications/HRNews/Pages/Powerof PositiveThinking.aspx.

"In fact, NYU Stern School of Business professor Jonathan Haidt wanted to find out...." Haidt, J. (2002). It's more fun to work on strengths than weaknesses (but it may not be better for you). Manuscript retrieved from http://people.virginia.edu/~jdh6n/strengths_analysis.doc.

"'Crowdsource your performance reviews,' says Eric Mosley . . ." Mosley, E. (2012). Crowdsource your performance reviews. *HBR Blog Network*. Retrieved from http://blogs.hbr.org/cs/2012/06/crowdsource_your _performance_r.html.

2. Don't Make Goals Easy and Vague

"'Challenging goals facilitate pride in accomplishment,' says goals researcher Gary Latham . . ." Latham, G. (2000). Motivate employee performance through goal setting. *Handbook of Principles of Organizational Behavior, 107*, 119.

"When employees are learning a new task, asking them to 'do their best' results in higher performance . . ." Latham, G. P., & Seijts, G. H. (1999). The effects of proximal and distal goals on performance on a moderately complex task. *Journal of Organizational Behavior, 20(4)*, 421–429; Seijts, G. H., & Latham, G. P. (2001). The effect of distal learning, outcome, and proximal goals on a moderately complex task. *Journal of Organizational Behavior, 22(3)*, 291–307.

3. Preview, Don't Just Review, Performance

"University of Missouri psychologist Laura King has found that writing about what you hope to accomplish . . ." King, L. A. (2001). The health benefits of writing about life goals. *Personality and Social Psychology Bulletin, 27*, 798–807.

"University of California, Los Angeles, psychologists Shelley Taylor and Lien Pham asked college students to visualize . . ." Pham, L. B., & Taylor, S. E. (1999). From thought to action: Effects of process-versus outcome-based mental simulations on performance. *Personality and Social Psychology Bulletin, 25(2)*, 250–260.

4. Chew the Fat; Don't Chew Them Out

"Frequent feedback has been shown over and over to be more effective than less frequent feedback." Bandura, A., & Schunk, D. H. (1981). Cultivating competence, self-efficacy, and intrinsic interest through proximal self-motivation. *Journal of Personality and Social Psychology, 41(3)*, 586.

CHAPTER 8: MEETINGS:
FROM ENERGY BUSTER TO ENERGY BOOSTER

Introduction

"...11 million meetings..." As cited in Cohen, M. A., Rogelberg, S. G., Allen, J. A., & Luong, A. (2011). Meeting design characteristics and attendee perceptions of staff/team meeting quality, *Group Dynamics: Theory, Research, and Practice, 15(1)*, 90–104.

"The National Statistics Council reports that people spend 37 percent of their time in meetings." As cited in Verizon Conferencing (1998). *Meetings in America: A Verizon Conferencing white paper*. Retrieved from https://e-meetings.verizonbusiness.com/global/en/meetingsinamerica/uswhite paper.php#COST.

"Another report calculates meeting time by size of company . . ." As cited in Cohen et al. (2011).

1. Start with a Sizzle

"In fact, 91 percent of attendees admit to daydreaming during meetings." Verizon Conferencing (1998). *Meetings in America: A Verizon Conferencing white paper*. Retrieved from https://e-meetings.verizonbusiness.com /global/en/meetingsinamerica/uswhitepaper.php#COST.

"University of North Carolina psychologist Barbara Fredrickson has found that positive emotions such as enthusiasm and interest serve two functions..." Fredrickson, B. L. (2001). The role of positive emotions in positive psychology: The broaden-and-build theory of positive emotions. *American Psychologist, 56(3)*, 218.

"Losada and his researchers observed 60 business teams in strategic planning meetings." Losada, M. (1999). The complex dynamics of high performance teams. *Mathematical and Computer Modelling: An International Journal, 30(9–10)*, 179–192; Fredrickson, B. L., & Losada, M. F. (2005). Positive affect and the complex dynamics of human flourishing. *American Psychologist, 60(7)*, 678.

"What Gifts and Music Can Do." Liver diagnosis test as cited in Seligman, M. (2002). *Authentic happiness: Using the new positive psychology to realize your potential for lasting fulfillment*. New York: Free Press.

2. Practice the Peak-End Rule

"Daniel Kahneman, Princeton University psychologist and Nobel Prize winner, ran a series of studies to learn how people evaluate past experiences."

Kahneman, D. (2011). *Thinking, fast and slow*. New York: Farrar, Straus and Giroux.

"Reminding ourselves why we're in this business, let's tell positive stories ...'" Conley, C. Personal interview. December 27, 2012.

3. Play Your Whole Bench

"An overwhelming majority of meeting attendees (92 percent) believe meetings have the potential to be a wonderful place to contribute. . . ," Verizon Conferencing (1998). *Meetings in America: A Verizon Conferencing white paper*. Retrieved from https://e-meetings.verizonbusiness.com/global/en/meetingsinamerica/uswhitepaper.php#COST.

"He discovered that high-performing teams had a 1:1 ratio between how many *questions* they asked and how much *information* they shared." Fredrickson, B. L., & Losada, M. F. (2005). Positive affect and the complex dynamics of human flourishing. *American Psychologist, 60(7),* 678.

CHAPTER 9: THE POSITIVE DEVIANT:
NO BUDGET? NO PROBLEM

"Goals researchers have found that people are more likely to achieve their goals when they break them into smaller subgoals or discrete steps." Bandura, A., & Schunk, D. H. (1981). Cultivating competence, self-efficacy, and intrinsic interest through proximal self-motivation. *Journal of Personality and Social Psychology, 41(3),* 586.

Reading and Discussion Guide

INTRODUCTION—YOU'VE TRIED EVERYTHING.
NOW TRY SOMETHING THAT WORKS

Whether you lead 3 employees or 3,000, *Profit from the Positive* is for business leaders who have already reaped the productivity gains from traditional improvement efforts such as Lean Six Sigma and are looking for additional tested methods to grow, improve, and transform their businesses.

We translate findings from the new science of positive psychology into clear actionable tools that can be applied immediately without spending a dime or hiring an expensive consulting company. So what is positive psychology?

First, let's be clear about what it is not: positive psychology is *not* positive thinking. Positive psychology researchers study topics such as productivity, resilience, motivation, emotions, strengths, team dynamics, and more. They seek answers to questions every business leader wrestles with: How can I increase productivity without adding to staff? How can I get my team to collaborate and step up its game? How can I motivate people to perform their very best?

Profit from the Positive is a practical guide for business leaders, managers, executive coaches, and human resource professionals.

Group Discussion Question

1. What do we hope to gain by reading *Profit from the Positive*?

PART I—IT'S ABOUT THE LEADER

CHAPTER 1—THE PRODUCTIVE LEADER: IT'S MORE THAN TIME MANAGEMENT

One of our clients, Eddie, used to check email, send text messages, and tweet—all while participating in a conference call. He believed that multitasking made him more productive. Wrong. Learn how flip-flop costs eat away at your productivity, decreasing it by more than 40 percent. In this chapter, we give you four evidence-based tools to make you a more productive leader without working more hours. First, don't "just do it," as Nike advises. Contrary to the popular slogan, research shows you'll boost your productivity if you "just plan it" instead. Second, find out how the Zeigarnik effect can help you stop procrastinating and avoid the perfectionist syndrome. Third, we're all taught in business school that setting SMART goals improves performance. Forget it. We've got the evidence for why you should set habits, not just goals. Think about habits as outsourcing some of your work to the automatic part of your brain. Fourth, work less to accomplish more. Successful companies such as Sony have figured out that workers are actually more productive and avoid burnout when they take more frequent breaks, unplug from email, and take time off. Being a highly productive leader is more than simply practicing good time management techniques. It's about creating a mindset, and in this chapter we show you how.

Group Discussion Questions

1. What's one best practice each of us can share on what we do today to boost our own productivity? Consuming large amounts of caffeine does not count.
2. What's one goal we could turn into a habit?
3. What are some ways we could work less and accomplish more?

CHAPTER 2—THE RESILIENT LEADER:
GIVE YOURSELF A PSYCHOLOGICAL
KICK IN THE PANTS

It's not enough to be a productive leader. You must also be a resilient leader to get others to follow you. We all experience setbacks now and then, such as losing a key customer account, flubbing a presentation to senior management, and being passed over for a promotion. But how quickly we bounce back from negative events is what separates an average leader from a great one. "If you want to be inventive, you have to be willing to fail," says Amazon founder and CEO Jeff Bezos. The world's largest online retailer has had its share of failures: hiring expensive editors to write book reviews, starting an auction business, and so on. But unlike Bezos, most of us avoid failures like the plague, and when we do fail, we beat ourselves up. In this chapter, learn how to give yourself a psychological kick in the pants by changing not what you do but how you think. The three tools, as demonstrated in hundreds of studies, are to stop being an expert, put on your explorer's hat, and win debates against yourself.

Group Discussion Questions

1. Where does believing we are the experts get us in trouble?
2. What's a self-limiting perspective we hold, and how could we replace it with a more empowering perspective?

CHAPTER 3—THE CONTAGIOUS LEADER:
CONTROL YOUR EMOTIONS, NOT YOUR EMPLOYEES

You may already be a productive leader, maybe even a resilient leader, but did you know you must also recognize that you are a contagious leader? Why? Because germs and colds aren't the only things we spread in the workplace. Our emotions, both positive and negative, are just as contagious. This spreading of emotions from one person to the next is what we call the *Achoo! effect*. But guess whose emotions are most contagious? The boss's. So what? Researchers have found that teams get more work done when the boss is in a good mood. Unfortunately, the reverse is true when the boss is in a foul mood. Cindi Bigelow, president of Bigelow Tea, sums it up this way: "Leaders cannot afford the luxury of a negative mood." In this chapter, you'll learn simple proven techniques to neutralize a negative mood. We also show you how to manage your control freak tendencies, which can get in the way of not only your productivity but that of your team.

Group Discussion Questions

1. Did anyone recognize himself or herself as an Oscar the Grouch?
2. Do any of us tend to micromanage? How can we help each other combat this tendency?
3. How can we give each other honest and constructive feedback about how we're perceived by others without getting defensive?

CHAPTER 4—THE STRENGTHS-BASED LEADER: CAPITALIZE ON WHAT'S RIGHT

Now that you've mastered the behaviors of the productive, resilient, and contagious leader, there's one more attribute you must cultivate to be successful. Visionary? Nope. Innovative? Not quite. Charismatic? Not even close. We call it the *strengths-based mindset*. Focusing on strengths, or what's working well, may sound easy, but in reality it's not. For many of us, our default action is to problem-solve. "My role is to analyze what's not working and then find solutions to turn things around," says one of our clients. "Isn't that what I'm paid to do?" In this chapter, we show you how to add to your arsenal of problem-solving skills by mining your own company for what's going right as the auto giant Toyota has done. It's all about the questions you ask. We also demonstrate how you can increase your team's performance by nearly 40 percent simply by the way you react to bad news. Third, we give you a three-minute no-cost way to uncover your own strengths.

Group Discussion Questions

1. How did we all score on the manager self-assessment in Appendix B: Is a Strengths-Based Approach a Good Fit for Me?
2. What are some things we already do that would be considered a strengths-based approach?
3. Which of our business practices could we bring even more of a strengths-based approach to?

PART II—IT'S ABOUT THE TEAM

CHAPTER 5—HIRING: THE FITNESS TEST

"He had all the right skills and experience, but he just didn't work out." Tired of spending big bucks on recruiting firms? Tired of starting the recruiting process all over again when your superstars fail to shine? Need to hire a team fast for the new business you are launching? Hiring mistakes can cost a company 15 times the employee's salary. In this chapter, we show you how to avoid costly mistakes by hiring for what's not on the resume. Additionally, there's a lot you can learn from companies large and small to ensure that your next hiring decision is a great one. From Rackspace's 10-hour interviews, to Google's "Googly" test, to Zappos.com's "How weird are you?" question, we summarize these best practices and show you how to implement them today.

Group Discussion Questions

1. What would our version of a fitness test look like?
2. What are three company or department values that make us successful? What questions should we ask job candidates to see if they would fit in?
3. Let's pick a job we know we will need to fill shortly or in the near future. What are the three most important attributes or interpersonal skills needed to be successful in this job that go beyond technical skills, education, and experience? What three

questions would we ask to see if a candidate possesses these skills?

CHAPTER 6—ENGAGING EMPLOYEES: BRING OUT THE BEST VERSUS GET THE MOST

A CIO we work with was curious. He wanted to know why only some of his teams complete their projects on time and on budget and seem to enjoy their work more than others. In particular, he wanted to know if teams were more engaged and productive when led by an optimistic manager. We conducted a study to find out. What was the secret ingredient? Optimism? No. It was FRE: Frequent Recognition and Encouragement. In this chapter, we bring you original research that shows that FRE is indeed free to implement and increases performance by over 40 percent. Find out how Zappos.com and other successful companies use FRE. We also show you how to turn strengths into a team sport and turn around poor performance by using a simple visual framework that will result in a more energized workforce.

Group Discussion Questions

1. What are some ways we could introduce strengths to our employees?
2. What are some things we do today to recognize our employees? What else could we do that's not another "program"?
3. Who has tried using the flow model to turn around an employee's performance? How well did it work?

CHAPTER 7—PERFORMANCE REVIEWS: CHANGE 'EM OR CHUCK 'EM

We're not sure who dreads performance reviews more: the manager, the employee, or HR. But managers really should be doing that dreaded performance review more rather than less frequently. Why? Because if done right, it can improve performance. In this chapter, we begin by exposing the flaws in the rating systems most businesses use today. For example, we shouldn't just be reviewing performance. We should be previewing it. Find out how to apply what sports psychologists have been doing with athletes for decades. You'll also discover how to improve overall performance by over a third simply by focusing more on what an employee does well than on what she needs to improve. Find out what managers and employees at companies as diverse as Great Harvest, Mozilla, and Unum have done to revamp the dreaded performance review.

Group Discussion Questions

1. What's working about our performance management process today? What do we need to change?
2. What methods do we use today to collect performance feedback? What else should we do to be sure feedback is balanced and more frequent?
3. How can we set goals differently this year so that they produce the right results?

CHAPTER 8—MEETINGS: FROM ENERGY BUSTER TO ENERGY BOOSTER

When our client Gloria first came to us, she described a typical day: "I practically live in meetings. From the time I arrive in the morning until the time I leave, I am in back-to-back meetings. Sometimes I'm double- and triple-booked." In this chapter, you will learn ways to stop the meeting madness that eats away at not only your time but your energy. First, avoid having your next meeting turn into a gripe session by using the magic ratio. Second, learn how to apply the peak-end rule to boost the energy in your next meeting. Third, learn how to play your whole bench.

Group Discussion Questions

1. How would we rate our own meetings using the 3:1 magic ratio?
2. Are there any meetings we could eliminate or reduce in length or frequency?
3. What can we do to start and end our meetings on a positive note?
4. What are some things we could do to improve meetings in which we're not the leader?

PART III—PUTTING IT ALL TOGETHER

CHAPTER 9—THE POSITIVE DEVIANT: NO BUDGET? NO PROBLEM

In the last chapter, we weave together everything about you as the leader from Part I and everything about leading your team from Part II. But let's be honest. As you begin to implement the content in *Profit from the Positive*, you may run into some resistance. Learn how to be a positive deviant from the dozens of companies and hundreds of business leaders and their teams that have successfully implemented our research-backed and tested advice. You don't need to be an expert, have a budget, or get your boss's permission to implement the tested tools in *Profit from the Positive*. You can be a positive deviant without anyone ever knowing it and profit from the positive.

Group Discussion Questions

1. Which tools really resonated with us that we can begin implementing today?
2. What are some other tools that may take us a bit more time to fully implement?
3. What are the FRESH themes in *Profit from the Positive*, and how might we use them to educate others?
4. What kinds of resistance can we expect from others, and how will we address it?

Acknowledgments

Thank you to the following colleagues, family members, and friends who helped bring *Profit from the Positive* from a half-baked idea to the finished product in your hands:

Nancy Ancowitz, Dana Arakawa, Scott Asalone, Kris Bertoldi, Kathryn Britton, Ann and Steven Charbonneau, Charlene Glidden, Carolyn, Maegan, and Neal Greenberg, Gina Greenlee, Nicholas Hall, James Harb, Paddy Hirsch, Stephanie Hsieh, Carol Huffman, Ronna-Renee Jackson, Bob Mauterstock, Tim Maynard, Michelle Mazzarella, Zak, Zina, Phil, Allan, and Dan Maymin, Peter McDonald, Rashmi Menon, Tina Merrill, Zach Nelson, Jill O'Brien, Kathy Owen, Gordon Parry, David J. Pollay, Jaime Raijman, Jason Ranucci, Tom Rath, Mhayse Samalya, Daniel Saul, Jan Stanley, Mark Testa, Greg Tranter, Doug Turner, Dan Tzur, and Scott Utzinger.

We wish to extend a special thank you to our agent, Jill Marsal of Marsal Lyon Literary Agency, and our editor, Casey Ebro at McGraw-Hill, both of whom believed in us and worked so hard on our behalf. Additionally, a big shout out to our wonderful team at McGraw-Hill: Pattie Amoroso, Stacey Ashton, Tara Cibelli, Dannalie Diaz, Mary Glenn, Maureen Harper, George Hoare, Ashley Lau, Eric Lowenkron, Ron Martirano, Amina Mehmedagic, Ty Nowicki, Mark Patterson, Pamela Peterson, Keith Pfeffer, Laura Yieh, Lydia Rinaldi, and others who contributed greatly behind the scenes.

Lastly and most crucially, we thank all of our positive deviants: the executives, managers, entrepreneurs, and teams we have coached over the years who were the first to implement the research-based tools that made it into *Profit from the Positive*.

Index

About the Authors

Margaret H. Greenberg is the president of The Greenberg Group, a consulting firm founded in 1997, after a 15-year career in corporate HR. Greenberg coaches Fortune 500 executives, primarily in the financial services sector, and their teams to achieve more than they ever thought possible. A pioneer in the field of applied positive psychology, Greenberg also designs and leads workshops and conferences for business audiences and is an expert on creating strengths-based organizations. She earned her BA in sociology from the University of Hartford and Master of Applied Positive Psychology degree from the University of Pennsylvania. Greenberg lives in Connecticut with her husband and two dogs. They have two grown daughters. For more information, please visit www.thegreenberggroup.org.

Senia Maymin is featured as a positive psychology executive coach in the media, including on PBS's *This Emotional Life*. When entrepreneurs and executives seek far-reaching productivity improvements, they call on Maymin as an executive coach and workshop leader. Maymin founded and is editor in chief of a research news website featuring more than 1,000 articles by over 100 authors. Additionally, Maymin manages a network of coaches that specialize in positive psychology methods. She has worked in finance on Wall Street and in technology as cofounder and president of two start-ups. Maymin holds a BA in math and economics from

Harvard, a Masters of Applied Positive Psychology from the University of Pennsylvania, and an MBA and PhD in organizational behavior from the Stanford Graduate School of Business. She speaks Russian, French, and Japanese. She lives with her family in California. For more information, visit the research news website at www.PositivePsychologyNews.com, the coaches network at positivecoaches.net and Maymin's website at www.senia.com.

CONTACT THE AUTHORS

Margaret and Senia would be delighted to hear from you:

Email: book@ProfitFromThePositive.com

Website: ProfitFromThePositive.com

Twitter: @profitbook

Facebook: https://www.facebook.com/ProfitFromThePositive